T0366467

Why Me?

ACKNOWLEDGMENTS

It is impossible to thank all who have helped make this book a reality, but a few deserve special mention. I should like to thank the Graduate School at Northern Illinois University for a Summer Grant that allowed uninterrupted weeks of writing; and Herman Stark, Frank Gonzalez, and Craig Hulfachor for reading parts of the manuscript as they were in process. I should also like to thank my sister, Dr. Fran Mayeski, my nephew Dr. Michael Degnan, and my friend, Christopher Morgan, for the kind of personal support that is so hard to define but is so precious; and my thanks to Debbie Sanderson for typing the manuscript under such trying circumstances.

Why Me?

PART ONE

RAISING

THE

QUESTION

. . .

PROLOGUE

Why me? The question is wrenched out in agony. It escapes unbidden, in bewilderment and wonder. It is more a demand than a question, perhaps more a cry of spirit than a weighing of intellect. Though it is presented as a private query, the demand is made for all when any endures its naked inquisition. It is not a whimper but a cosmic assault on thinking, forged not in pity but in outrage. Why me?

It seems that human understanding is never so bereft as when confronted by the curious fates that measure most of what we are. Why should this fair youth die so young or this beloved mother be marooned in distant paralysis; why is the passenger in 26A killed in the crash while the one in 26B escapes unharmed; why is this one so favored, that one so unlucky? Who, or what, is responsible for these draconian selections?

The cheerful mastery of our science, so confident in explaining all that happens, is mute and helpless before these idle turns of the dice. The agonies of undeserved misery no less than the merry favors of the fortunate seem simply beyond the canons of our thinking.

> Nature and Nature's laws
> lay hid in night;
> God said "Let Newton be!"
> and all was light.
> Alexander Pope, "Epitaph for Newton"

Does the poet say "all"? To be sure, Newton and his scientist followers can indeed show us the causes; we can make sense of what happens, for events, apparently, all have causes, and if we do not yet know exactly what the causes are, we know that they are there, waiting to be discovered. We often, at least, know how to calculate the odds. But what we do not know, what seems to lie beyond Newton's pool of light, is what it *means* to be selected by these fickle uncertainties. We may know how to think about caused events, but we do not seem to know how to think about who we are, the prey of the arbitrary. We call it luck, or fortune, or fate, or simply the way things are, but these are but names we give, like fig leaves to hide nakedness, to keep us from reflecting on the dire limits of the mind, to keep us from the abject terror of nihilistic despair.

It is better, it would seem, to dismiss such notions altogether than to try to think about them, for in confronting them our impotence embarrasses us. Such lofty and noble beings as ourselves should not be disarmed by these childish, unanswerable questions. In the arrogance of our success we children of Newton find our powers so diminished—even nugatory—that we are tempted to abandon all hope or reason. For what can we say to the child struck blind, the condemned who draws the shortest straw, the sufferer who does not deserve his pain? Are not our pious adages comforts only to us and not to those denounced by fortune?

What we *do not* understand can be remedied by study, but what we *cannot* understand is a threat to the range and integrity of our reason, perhaps even to the worth of our existence. But just exactly what is it that we are asking when we demand a response to "why me?" Perhaps this is the greatest philosophical question we can ask. It is, to be sure, rarely asked by those who consider themselves philosophers, possibly because the degree of courage and wisdom to confront it surpasses our meager resources. What are we asking *about* when this dreadful demand is raised? This is what we must now consider.

But if so, it is no mean task. Our very natures seem to rebel against us, for there is solace in avoiding questions that menace the trust in established canons of thought. Yet it is also our natures that demand we carry on. At the very least we want to know if the question itself makes sense.

What is one asking when demanding "why me?" It must first be made clear that any reasonable response to a question of this sort must not only provide a coherent account but must also confront why the question is asked. One may ask why the authorities arrest unlicensed drivers and be told it is because such drivers are breaking the law or because policemen are sworn to uphold the statutes. But, although such an answer provides a coherent response, the question itself has not been confronted. We want to know why there is such a law. Or if someone asks why a bully beats a child and is told that the reason is the bully's superior strength, we admit the relevance of the answer but do not accept it as a response. The question "why me?" cannot therefore be answered by any account that merely explains what or how things happen.

But these examples are misleading to some extent. Usually the question "why?" raises a purposive account: we license drivers to control public safety, bullies beat up on children in order to satisfy their base gratifications of arrogance and self-importance. But the term 'why' in the fate-question "why me?" is not a purposive one, though many established philosophical accounts assume it to be one and respond, erroneously, by providing a purposive explanation. What the question really asks, as this inquiry will uncover, is not, "for what purpose was I selected to endure undeserved suffering or undeserved happiness?" but quite simply, "how am I to *think* about myself as a fated being?" It is the profound difficulty in isolating this response that makes this question so thorny and elusive.

In this inquiry, however, the procedure demands that we

approach the question more cautiously, and hence we must plot the development of the question from its more instinctive beginning. In the first instance it seems we are asking, "why should undeserved misfortunes happen to me?" That is, the question concerns the origin and meaning of fated *events* and why *I* should have to suffer them rather than someone else. In this we question fate in its selective sense. We wonder if there are reasons, causes, principles of retribution or warning, trials to test or strengthen character, or even some grand and cosmic plan that would somehow make sense of my having to endure what others do not. Even if we reject the naive accounts, we still wonder if there are any grounds for being a victim of unearned punishment. We might also *then* wonder why such misfortunes occur at all, not just to me but to anyone. Does our existence make sense if so much of it is arbitrary?

We might also question why we are favored by good fortune, but this seems less urgent. Nevertheless, the philosophical account of how we think about misfortune should also apply to the pleasant and generous bestowals of fate. And so in this first instance we ask first, "why should unearned fortune, either good or bad, happen to *me*," and then, on a more reflective level, "why should such things happen at all?" This might be called the 'fate of our events', and as the first it has a special status in the questioning of 'why me?'

In the second or deeper instance, however, we may realize that there is another way to address this question of fate: "why is there a 'me' at all?" The question is not merely "why does this happen to me?" but also "why should there be someone like me whatsoever?" I did not choose to be born, nor did I have any input into the circumstances, heritage, tradition, or parentage that go to make up who I am. Of course, further reflection reveals that I would have to exist already in order to be asked if I wanted to exist, so the question seems formally ridiculous; but this bit of cleverness cannot dissuade us entirely from wondering about such things. Unlike the first instance, which asks why certain things happen to me, the second instance of the fate question may be more fundamental. Perhaps if I were to know how to think about why *I* exist at all, I might be able to give some response to the question of why certain unearned things happen to me rather than to others.

The third instance of the fate question is the deepest. Why should there be *anything* whatsoever. Here the question of fate is plunged to its most fundamental and irresistible level. "Why me?" becomes "why *be* at all?" We are faced with the ultimate question.

But even in the first instance we realize that part of the questioning depends on the awareness that there can be no answer that would explain the anguish away. A certain degree of simple acceptance must be assumed lest in making demands for so much clarity we thereby erode all possibility of life, self, and history. There is no answer that will provide complete solace to the victim of cruel fortune, for then there would be no fortune. It is essential that we keep this in mind, for in seeking to give answers too quickly we may eclipse the question altogether. Realizing that the question "why me?" is in reality four questions, (1) "why do unearned events happen to *me*?" (2) "why do they happen *at all*?" (3) "why is there a *me* in the first place?" and (4) "why should *anything be* at all?" we realize the question of fate is far deeper and far more fundamental than may at first seem possible. When we conjoin with this the further realization that any answer that explains fate *away* renders the entire interrogation invalid, the *density* then of this haunting question may be enough to frighten away the timid among the would-be inquirers.

Nevertheless, we are not entirely without *some* resources. Instinctively, when we think of fate or destiny we tend to focus upon the great myths, dark in the distant origins of our culture. Perhaps above all we think of the early Greeks and their vague and even inconsistent myths about Moira, that impersonal force of both natural necessity and moral hegemony governing the lives not only of men but also of the gods. We may recall the scholars telling us about how the gods and heroes were forced to yield to her blind imperatives. Homer seemed convinced that Moira could never be superseded even by the gods, but Hesiod sometimes speaks of gods and even men occasionally as briefly violating her precepts, though such violations always resulted in severe reprisals. Yet Moira is not herself a god; she is more a cosmic and moral force, and her dominance over the gods tells us more about polytheism and the necessarily less-than-infinite divinities that make up such wondrous stories than it does about fate. The very inconsistency and vagueness about her powers may well mirror our own confusion and how we think about fate.

Yet we may find some hints in the more recent Teutonic myths, especially as dramatized by Richard Wagner. In his opera *Götterdämmerung*, we learn of the three Norns, the daughters of the all-knowing but curiously impotent Erda, who continuously weave the great rope of fate, until the hero Siegfried, through his heroic act of rebellion, forces the rope to be broken, thereby rendering the Norns superfluous and distracted. Such myths, whether Greek or Teutonic, are not without interest, and their murky stories seem to reflect how we do in fact think about such things.

Yet these are ancient stories; we must rely on classical scholars to tell us what they mean. No modern thinker believes literally in these mythical accounts, and indeed to *appeal* to them in a serious way, aside from our own legitimate fascination for our mythical origins, is simply unacceptable. They may help us understand the ancients, but they no longer suffice to make sense of our daily lives, and they especially do not serve us in the present quest. For we do not seek to know how prescientific cultures accounted for the seeming randomness of chance events; we want to know how to think about what these things can possibly mean to the sophisticated or at least modern mind. When outraged by the unfairness of seemingly irrational violations of sense and planning, there is neither solace nor enlightenment to be found in scholarly accounts of ancient myth.

This inquiry is not in any way meant to provide a scholarly analysis of mythology. Though these ancient stories are truly fascinating and deserve the extensive scholarship available to the student of antiquity, it is an embarrassment, one might even say a scandal, that our only resource is myth when we seek to probe into what it means for an enlightened person to be confounded by the fickle decrees of fortuity. Indeed, too much fascination with mythical accounts of fate may actually distract from the honesty and boldness necessary to discover how an acceptable way of thinking about these curious influences can be found. Accordingly, in this inquiry any analysis of mythology and the wonderful resources of the classical scholars who explain these myths is eschewed utterly. This may irritate some readers, but there are some great advantages to this method, for by the excise of mythological scholarship both emphasis and attention are directed to the poignancy and inescapable relevance of the question "why me?"

But this rejection of the mythical accounts of fate, doubtless lamentable to many readers, raises a deep and possibly frustrating question. If we delete the myths, have we not also deleted the question entirely? In other words, must we not consider the possibility that notions such as fate, destiny, and chance are entirely mythical, so that in putting the myths aside we have put the *problem* aside as well? Perhaps without myth there is no meaning to fate. Perhaps fate is an entirely meaningless notion. This question therefore deserves the first serious consideration: is fate meaningful at all?

1

. . .

THE RANGE
OF THE QUESTION

IS FATE AN EMPTY NOTION?

The first question that must be raised is whether the concept of fate is even intelligible. It is by no means unprecedented that we should employ terms and even search after the meanings of concepts that careful philosophical analysis renders totally empty and unthinkable. Perhaps fate appears both troublesome and mysterious simply because it is an illegitimate notion. This possibility must be examined.

. . .

One way to test this is to consider whether the appearance of the term makes any difference in a sentence.

a. All men die.
b. All men are fated to die.

Does the second sentence tell us anything that the first does not? Or do the words "are fated to" merely add stylistic intensification of the fact? Upon analysis it may seem that the second sentence is merely a restatement of the first because it is difficult to identify exactly what the second asserts that is not already stated in the first. Does the second tell us something that is in the world? Does it inform us that dying is to be understood in a special way? Certainly both sentences seem to reveal the same fact. If one argues that the second is reducible to the first there is then a very good reason for questioning whether fate is meaningful at all.

We often react to the troubling occurrences in our lives that seem to provoke an appeal to the concept 'fate' by emphasizing the powerlessness of our thinking and control. One will often say, "That's just the way it is," when confronted with an inexplicable grief or circumstance. To say this, however, is to assert that one can only accept what happens as an event and that explanations as to 'how' or 'why' simply are not available. "Such things just happen" means that the world contains some events that can be known but not understood. The term 'just' in both of these colloquial sentences is a limiting term; it bars us from further analysis or thinking.

But if we are compelled to say of any event that it cannot be questioned, that the brute fact of its occurrence is all that remains open to us, then the second sentence above truly adds nothing to the first, except perhaps to emphasize that what is said in the first is all we can expect to know. Such awareness is of little comfort to one beset by grief and puzzlement, though it may serve to deter the sufferer from hopeless questioning and possibly even from a false assignment of undeserved guilt. But in any event, these reflections diminish considerably the range of inquiry into the meaning of fate, for they suggest that fate has at best a minimal degree of thinkability. Rather than being a great question, it is a trivial one. What we mean by fate is simply that things happen—not an inspired discovery.

This deflating of the meaning and importance of fate is by no means without noble support. In *The Critique of Pure Reason* (A85/B117) Immanuel Kant argues that 'fate', as well as kindred notions such as 'luck' and 'fortune' are 'usurpatory concepts', a compelling description meaning that such terms look like concepts and seem to function like concepts but in fact are mere usurpers, and hence do not explain anything. Kant's point, which is surely valid, can be seen by once again contrasting two sentences:

c. "The rain caused the river to rise."
d. "The general arrived at the crucial time and place on the battlefield by sheer luck."

The first of these sentences is, according to the Kantian analysis, an entirely legitimate explanation, but the second is not. It may be thought that rain is a cause of the river's rising, but luck or fate cannot be seen as a cause of the general's arriving at the crucial spot on the battlefield. Sentences (c) and (d) do seem similar, however, and it is easy to see why a casual or uncritical reading of (d) may lead us to believe that luck or fate does actually explain. This is why Kant calls such terms 'usurpatory concepts'. But usurpers must be deposed and replaced with the true and proper authority. Again it seems that the appeal to fate in (d) is merely an acceptance that the event took place, but by using the term 'luck' or 'fate' we bar any further explanative account. So 'fate' seems to mean little more than *that* something occurs, with the dubious addendum that such occurrence cannot be explained causally. It must be noted, however, that although Kant identifies fate as a usurpatory concept, he himself uses the term in a most powerful way in the opening sentence of *The Critique of Pure Reason*, in which he asserts that "human reason is endowed with this peculiar fate," that it cannot resist raising the very metaphysical questions it cannot answer. Is this a gross inconsistency? Kant's injunction against fate is that it is sometimes falsely used as a concept, as in the case of 'luck' in the above example. But he does not prohibit the use of such terms altogether. When his famous opening sentence of the *Critique* appeals to fate, it is not as an *explanation* but simply as something that seems to be a part of our nature—perhaps so deep and essential a part of our nature that we cannot explain it but simply accept it. Kant surely is correct that fate is not an explanatory concept, yet he himself uses the term in a serious, indeed profound, way.

■   ■   ■

But if fate is not an explanatory concept, what is it? When we speak of fate we seem to imply some kind of inevitability or irresistibility, suggesting there is nothing we can do to alter what occurs. Perhaps the comparison should be:

  e. All men must die.
  f. All men are fated to die.

Is there anything in sentence (f) that is not already contained in (e)? This point is more obvious if we substitute 'mortals' for 'men', making (e) an analytic proposition. To say of something that it is fated is to say it had to happen. All men, by their very nature, are mortal and hence must die, so we say, "It is their fate," meaning, "it is due to their natures."

If this analysis is correct, fate means little more than a modal operator and is no more mysterious than the formal distinction between necessity and contingency. To be sure, this is an advance on the first analysis, because it does give to fate a meaning beyond that of a mere factual occurrence; but fate is still replaceable, by the terms 'must' or 'because of the nature of the thing'. If fate is genuinely replaceable by these formalist notions, again the analysis leaves very little to be investigated.

But neither the first nor the second of these analyses seems to cover all of what is meant by 'fate'. One element in our understanding of this term is that by 'fate' is meant that which is neither controllable nor understandable. But if this is what is entailed in the concept, and if there are uses of the term that are not reducible to either factual claims or necessary claims based on the analysis of the nature of the concept, then a more serious question must be raised.

IS FATE A THREAT TO REASON?

One of the most revered maxims in philosophy is that nothing is without a reason. In its classical formulation this maxim is known as the principle of sufficient reason: *nihil est sine ratio*. To appeal to fate, however, seems to contradict this principle, for if 'fate' is not an explanatory concept it seems it cannot qualify as a *reason*. We can and do give causal accounts of our undeserved misfortunes as well as our inherited destinies, but such accounts do not answer the question we want to know. If we say, for example, that it is simply my fate to be born American, we do not deny that causal accounts can be given for my birth; but we deny that these accounts in any way explain why it should be *me* who has been so favored. There is thus something I want to know (why am I so lucky?) that cannot be answered by causal accounts but that still demands some response. Because I am unable to give it, I must abandon the universality of the principle of sufficient reason; it is to say that not everything is caused, perhaps even that not all is intelligible. This is unacceptable, for if fate refers to what cannot be thought about, then to think is no more successful than not to think.

Closer analysis reveals, however, that one need not succumb to misology merely because we seem to be able to use the term 'fate' in a meaningful way. To say that there is a reason for everything is not to say we are aware of such reasons. This seems to make fate the same as our ignorance. To say we are fated to do or to be something is simply to say we are ignorant of the causes, not that there are no causes.

A family takes a climbing hike on a mountain and all are killed when a landslide buries them. To describe their deaths as fateful is simply to say they are unaware of the causes. They did not know of the geological conditions that brought about the landslide. Had they known of the unstable conditions of the ice and rock they would not have chosen that time and place to hike and hence would not have been killed. Their

fate is their ignorance. The principle of sufficient reason asserts not that we will know of all the causes but simply that
there are causes. If fate is merely ignorance, then fate is no
threat whatsoever to the integrity and universality of rational
principles.

But does an appeal to the ignorance of the family really tell
us about their fate? Others were ignorant of the geological
conditions, but they did not die. Besides, what disturbs us
about this family tragedy is not that there were unknown
causes that brought about the slide but that it happened to be
this family. If ignorance of causes explains their fate, then all
who were ignorant should have had similar fates. What this
reflection seems to show is that neither knowledge nor ignorance of causes seems to reveal what is meant by fate. We are
concerned not with the cause of the landslide but with what
it means. Thus, one's appeal to fate does not threaten the
principle of sufficient reason, but then neither does our ignorance of these reasons suffice to illuminate what is meant
by fate or to alleviate the anguish of the question "why me?"

Yet this appeal to ignorance may still be a fruitful consideration. The family being crushed by the avalanche stuns us
because we do not seem to be able to give an adequate account of why this family had to suffer the loss of their lives
and why remaining friends and kin were burdened with grief.
Perhaps, some might tell us, these events have not only
causes but also meanings, which are known only to God. Perhaps, indeed, such untoward happenings are simply the will
of a divine providence who directs all things by a wisdom that
surpasses human understanding. Such an appeal may not be
logically contradictory, but even if it is accepted it does not
relieve us of the burning anguish that is inherent in the question of fate. A believer in theistic providence simply does not
believe in fate at all. Such a believer putatively knows perfectly well why these seeming misfortunes occur: because an
all-powerful deity has arranged for them to happen for our

own advantage, even though we do not see the benefit. Thus, for the believer, the event is neither unfortunate nor unknown, and hence cannot be fate at all. Inherent in such providential theism is the denial that such occurrences are in any sense bad or evil: they *seem* to be unfortunate but are really blessings in disguise. Such a theodicy, though provocative, forfeits our capacity to distinguish the ill from the fair, for in both we must perforce remain ignorant of the divine will. Is absolutely *everything* that happens ultimately for our own benefit? If so, then there is no difference at all, save a seeming one, between fortune and misfortune, and fate as a meaningful notion disappears. If not, then the defender of such theodicy is ill-prepared to explicate the difference.

There is a further possibility that may render fate a genuine threat to reason, and this is the rather fantastic belief that there exists a noncalculating, blind, and only occasionally interruptive force that, less than omnipotent but still influential, effects our lives—or some of our lives—with random but incomplete causal interference. To appeal to such a force is necessarily to appeal to the ultimately irrational, because there are no principles or rules that govern its influence and because there is no way of determining when or if this power is present. As incoherent as such a view may be, it is alarmingly prevalent among the superstitious and uncritical, who are woefully legion. Such a view would seriously threaten the integrity of reason and would lead us to misology.

IS FATE METAPHYSICAL NIHILISM?

It was considered earlier that fate may simply mean necessity, as when we say all men must die, that is, are fated to do so. These considerations were designed to illuminate the possibility that fate had no nonreducible meaning. It is possible, however, to develop this insight to a much higher level of generality and to consider the claim that fate—far from being

a mere meaningless term or even a misological threat to reason—is indeed a metaphysically nihilistic notion in which
whatever happens, whether foul or fair, is inevitable, pressing
fate to the extreme of fatalism. This view is entirely opposite
to the above persuasions, which see in fate that which is unintelligible; rather, fatalism makes everything that happens
entirely intelligible, indeed inevitable. The loftiest claims of
knowledge are those that are apodictic; and if all that happens
must happen, then knowledge of these principles would be a
priori. It is curious to reflect that a metaphysical view in
which perfect knowledge is obtainable just because reality is
perfectly coherent and lawlike is the one metaphysical view
that is most dreadful and terrifying. Perhaps, then, the goal
of perfect knowledge is not only of dubious worth but also of
ultimate and fundamental evil.

Fatalism must be distinguished from determinism; the
former is fundamentally a theory of truth, the latter a cosmological theory about entities and causes. Fatalism finds its
support in the notion that future claims can be true, determinism in the belief that the natural order of causal accounts
permits of no deviation or alternative. The ontological arguments for such theories do not concern us here, except in a
sketch to show the significance of fate. But the ramifications
of fatalism are indeed of critical interest for this inquiry. For
fatalism seems, in the offering of a perfectly coherent universe, to deny any autonomy to individual human beings, denying not only their freedom but also their meaning.

The classical or Greek view, however, seems innocent
enough at first reading. Whatever is true is grounded in the
real; that is, the way the world is makes sentences or beliefs
true. If the north pole is colder than the equator, then the
claim that asserts this is considered true because of the fact.
What could be more reasonable than this? Similarly, if tomorrow is to be colder than today, then, if I assert this today, what

makes my assertion true is the fact about tomorrow's temperature. Surely if the temperature on Tuesday is 40°F at noon and the temperature on Wednesday is 20°F at noon, then the claim made on Tuesday that tomorrow will be colder than today is true; and what *makes* it true is the colder temperature. Again this seems eminently reasonable. But if today's claim about tomorrow's temperature is true *now* because of what *will* be, then today's claim about the future is not merely likely but also true; and if it *is* true, then it *can*not be false. Whatever *cannot* be false, however, *must* be true, and hence tomorrow's temperature is already inevitable. Thus, because it seems to make sense to make futural claims and because nothing makes sense unless it can be true or false, then future-tense sentences are indeed possibly true, and, if this is so, then what *makes* them true is reality, so reality must be inevitable.

If we define a free act as one initiated by an agent for whom alternative possibilities are available and if everything is inevitable so that there are no alternative possibilities to what is the case, then there are no free acts. This seems a draconian conclusion to such an innocent premise, but the argumentation is compelling. Aristotle was so offended by this conclusion, yet so persuaded by the reasoning, that he was led to deny the premise, and hence he reasons that sentences about the future are neither true nor false.

The point that is of importance is human intelligibility. In order to make sense of human existence, the notion of responsibility must be presupposed. There can be no responsibility if whatever happens must happen, no more so than that there is responsibility for the lamp lighting the room. Faced with either future-tense sentences being true or people being free, it is easy to understand why Aristotle preferred the latter. But what does this argument do to our instincts about fate? If *some* of our affairs are fated, why are not all fated? If we want to say there is more to fate than what happens, then are we not left open either to an entirely random and incoherent universe in which only *some* things are capable of being thought about or to a grim, inevitable, and fatalistic universe in which not only is freedom impossible but also a meaningful autonomous existence? Either view seems unacceptable. Indeed, none of the above views account for fate, whether it is simply what happens, or what must happen, or what God wills, or simply what we do not know or what we cannot know. None seem to come to grips with the true meaning of fate. Though each of these may have a role to play in our understanding, none satisfy the inquiry.

This dissatisfaction with such accounts may be due in part to an uncertainty as to what is being asked; for it is not obvious that the question of fate is necessarily a metaphysical question. Certainly it is not a scientific question; that is, the search for fate is not a search for cause. But if the question is not a metaphysical or scientific question, what could it be?

IS FATE A MORAL NOTION?

The possibility of fatalism has raised the question of fate and freedom. Perhaps the proper approach to fate can be found by considering moral presuppositions. Analyses of ordinary, everyday uses of the term 'fate' seem to indicate that the term refers to whatever does not fall under the influence of human decision but is about human occurrence. Accordingly, because I have no control over the color of my eyes or who my parents are, but because I do seem to have control over much of my conduct—such as whether I should deceive my spouse or respect another's property—we seem to want to divide human activity into two realms, the free and the fated. By this division we then seem to imply that the term 'fate' is in contrast to the term 'freedom', thus giving it a peculiarly moral significance; to wit, I am responsible for what I freely do and not for what is fated. Such an account leaves unconsidered the metaphysical origins altogether and focuses solely on the availability of praise and censure. I should be praised or blamed for what I freely do; I should be neither blamed nor praised for those conditions of my life and person over which I have no influence. Thus, because I do not select the color of my eyes or the shape of my nose, I say they are simply fated to be what they are; but because I do select what I sign in contracts, such contracts are deemed my responsibility. To be sure, many would insist that such distinctions must have metaphysical presuppositions, and perhaps they do, but it is possible to inquire into the meanings of both fate and freedom without establishing these presuppositions; furthermore, it might be argued that it is metaphysics itself that is dubious, and not the moral judgments that we make quite readily and coherently in our daily affairs.

But of course this step, though perhaps clearing away some metaphysical debris, does not clarify but obfuscates. For the point is that responsible conduct seems capable of being thought about, whereas fated conditions, which seem to play an equal, if not larger, role in our lives, seem not to be able to be thought about. What makes freedom an interesting notion is the fact that I can make moral judgments, whereas the elements of fate are not so judged by the very analytic distinction just made. In order for the distinction between fate and freedom to be philosophically acceptable, both must be able to be thought about. But I can think about what is free only because I can judge morally; if such judgments cannot apply to fate, then the moral approach seems no more illuminating than the metaphysical. For it does us no good at all to say of fate simply that we cannot make moral judgments about it. We want to know how we *can* think about fate, not how we *cannot* think about it. Furthermore, to appeal to freedom as some kind of opposing, and hence illuminating, principle by which one can interrogate fate is to seek light from what is as dark as any notion in the philosophical reservoir. Freedom is itself as troubling as fate: both are profound and puzzling notions. It may well be, as this inquiry will, it is hoped, show, that the notions of fate and freedom are closely, even intimately, interrelated; but this merely shows we have much work to do; it cannot now be used as a technique for simplistic definition.

Raising the question in this way, however, has provoked a deeper and more fascinating problem. Is fate truly to be understood in terms of nonresponsibility? This would suggest that who I *am* is morally unthinkable, but what I *do* is morally thinkable. Might one not suggest the opposite? Perhaps most of our so-called responsible—hence free—actions stem from character. Do we really expect a kind and generous person, when asked for a donation by a hungry child, to turn the child down? Do we expect a mean and selfish person to bestow generous gifts? Perhaps, as Heraclitus suggests, our character is our fate. To suggest this in no way implies a denial of freedom but simply refocuses the target: one is free not in one's actions but toward one's character; that is, I am free to be *who* I am, and because of who I am I act in certain and particular ways. This Heraclitean suggestion is both seductive and repulsive, but it is always fascinating. How can I change who I am? On the one hand, if much of what constitutes my personality or character is inherited, then how can I be held responsible for it? On the other hand, surely freedom means very little if I am unable to be who I am as a result of some kind of responsibility for my character. But such reflections seem entirely alien to the traditional ways of thinking about such things. Perhaps it is better to accept the earlier suggestion that the term 'fate' is simply that about which one cannot think at all; it is a meaningless notion. This brings us to the final possibility of the ultimately unacceptable views about fate.

DOES FATE EXIST AT ALL?

"I do not believe in fate." This is a claim one often hears when considering our inquiry. But what is being denied in such a claim? Does the disbeliever doubt the existence of a preternatural intruder into human affairs? If this is what is meant, most thoughtful people may well agree. Does the disbeliever doubt that there is anything over which he has no control or that there is at least knowledge of causes? If this is meant, then that person is either remarkably naive or deeply self-deceived. Or does the person mean—and this is surely the most likely—that it is simply a hopeless question, that we simply do not know *how* to think about such things, and that by 'disbelief' what is really meant is 'disinterest'? For can anyone honestly deny that certain things happen that seem neither deserved nor defensible but that must be endured without too much questioning? If this is the point, then the phrase, "I do not believe in fate," actually means, "I do not want to think about such things because there seems to be no way to think about them successfully." If by 'fate' is meant the occurrence of things beyond our ken, then obviously fate exists. But to admit we cannot think about such things is an embarrassment to the esteem of the mind, and so we disregard them altogether.

What is it that we seek to understand? It has been noted that an appeal to fate is not an appeal to causes or to the ignorance of causes. Perhaps, then, these reflections on the possible realm of discourse in which fate should be considered has shown that there is no such realm at all. If neither science, nor metaphysics, nor moral reasoning provides us with a meaningful discipline in which to carry out the inquiry, then perhaps the first of our considerations is the right one: fate does not mean anything. And yet . . .

The man who draws the shortest straw is just unlucky. By

this we mean that we cannot explain why he among all the hostages had to die. That is why the method of drawing straws was selected. By leaving it to chance we remove the burden of choice. He knows he was selected not because he was in any way less worthy to live. Not wanting to select the scapegoat on the basis of moral reason, we deliberately choose to rely on a method that favors no one: sheer chance. To demand we can explain *why* he picked the shortest straw is to defeat the purpose of drawing straws altogether. Hence the demand for an explanation is irrational; it defeats the purpose of the procedure.

We deprive the man of his life by relying on sheer chance. Do we also deny him any rational resource *at all*? What do we tell him as he awaits the terrorist's bullet: just don't think about it? Why deprive him of his most precious right, his most dear aspect? The cruelty of truth is this: we must think about it.

But *how*? What, as we have asked above, is the realm of discourse? What is the provence of the inquiry? What do we want to know? The hostage who has drawn the shortest straw knows about causes; he knows quite well that the ignorance as to which straw was shortest was shared by all who had to select them. He knows there was no human malice in the selection, no deviation of the laws of nature. Yet he still makes the fierce and irresistible demand: "Why me?" Can we scan this more closely?

What the hostage wants to know is this: Is there any sense at all to my life? Is my misfortune capable of being thought about in any way whatsoever? Is my existence meaningful? If one were to tell my story, would the telling make sense? It is gross and indecent to deny the reality of misfortune; it is even worse to sequester it from the light of thought. Somewhere in the ample arena of human thinking there must be resources to illuminate this dire inevitability that seems more important than all the plans of human cunning, all the selections and options and choices of so-called free judgment. If we cannot tell this story meaningfully, if one's fortune is simply one's inexplicable and unexplainable lot, then why have we ever thought it worth our while to think at all?

HOW CAN FATE BE THOUGHT?

But a glimmer has already appeared in this story of the unfortunate hostage. We say that the captives had to surrender one of their own to be executed; not wanting to be burdened with selecting on the grounds of desert, they appealed to a simple device of chance to relieve them of an otherwise unendurable burden. Thus, for the captive men, it is seen as a benefit that chance offers them a way of avoiding an ever greater torment. They are glad that an appeal can be made to that which, by its very nature and meaning, cannot even be expected to yield any reasons or accounts. It is better, it seems, to rely upon fortune just because we cannot accept the huge weight of choosing beyond our ken. We have no right to choose which of us must die; for how would that selection be made? And so we are relieved by the possibility of appealing to unmeasured and random judgment. By leaving it to chance, or luck, or fortune, we avoid assuming the terrible mantle of God.

This is an unexpected nugget of gold. We do not want to play God. Why? Because we are not gods. To appeal to fate is thus to admit our finitude. But as we are indeed finite and in all honesty know that we lack sufficient wisdom to act as if we were divine, we take grateful refuge in the possibility of fate. It makes being finite *bearable*.

Fate is therefore not always an enemy but sometimes a friend to mankind. It at least saves us from having to assume divine and infinite responsibility. But does this relieve us of confronting the terrible question "why me?" It is but a nugget only, not the mother lode. Yet it is enough. It shows us that if we but broaden our search, there must be some veins or fault lines in the rock that would lead us to the fecund strata of precious ore. We have seen that the question cannot be resolved by making speculative leaps into metaphysics. (Perhaps no serious question can be answered this way.) The brief discussion of the captive hostages seeking a refuge from unacceptable responsibility in fate has revealed that perhaps the proper methodology would be to examine some of the various ways in which we actually *use* the notion of fate meaningfully. From the analysis of these realms we may be able to elicit the underlying principles or guiding notions that render them intelligible.

Who *uses* fate? By this I mean, who carries out meaningful activities in ways that rely upon the very mystery and arbitrariness of fate to accomplish their end? Various suggestions come to mind. The nonprofessional *gambler*, for one, takes delight and excitement in allowing sheer chance to grant him or to deprive him of valuable exchange. Perhaps a closer look at the gambler will reveal at least some hints as to how we think about chance and luck. But chance and luck seem more ephemeral than fate. The *historian* unfolds the telling of his people's story in such a way as to render the magnitude of seeming random forces into a coherent unity, a unity that reveals the destiny of his nation. Perhaps by analyzing how the historian accomplishes this, further clues may be discovered. Both the gambler and the historian seem to *use* fate to make their endeavors possible.

The *birthday celebrant* is likewise a fascinating figure; for in celebrating birthdays we rejoice in the occurrence of an event, which, though certainly caused and biologically explainable, remains a mystery to the extent that who one *is* as a result of this event surpasses its explanatory power. As common as birthdays may be, their philosophical significance is awesome, for if the second instance of the question "why me?" emphasizes the pronoun, then that *we* are born at all seems a wondrous fate. To the jaded, the study of celebrating birthdays may seem unduly parochial, even silly, but philosophers cannot be distracted by such idle contempt. Surely the concept 'that I am at all', which is what birthdays celebrate, belongs in the study of fate. Along with the gambler and the historian, the celebrant of birthdays reveals that a world in which fate plays a major role is somehow worthier of thought—and hence *can* be thought—than a world in which all is earned, knowable, and predictable.

Yet the greatest user of fate in human endeavors is none of these three but instead is the artist who renders fate into something magnificent, the tragedian. The other three assume fate, or presuppose it, or use it to their advantage, but the tragedian confronts it boldly; the tragedian grants to fate all of its terrors and mysteries, all of its torment and power, and yet trumpets its necessity as a triumph of who we are. By stripping fate naked on the stage, the tragic artist tortures the torturer, compelling fate to yield its secrets. For it is in tragedy that fate, in conquering, is magnificently overcome. The king, Oedipus, is brought down by his fate, but in the tragic art fate is mastered by *Oedipus the King*.

These four are remarkable resources: the gambler, the historian, the birthday celebrant, and the tragedian. There may be others, but these will serve. They are specimens beneath our microscope, but they also are sacraments, in a way, the exercise of which produces a reverence for who we are.

PART TWO

THE

FOUR

FIGURES

■   ■   ■

2

. . .

THE GAMBLER
Fate as Chance

The professional gambler, who in calculating the odds expects to win slightly more often than to lose and hence relies on this long-term constancy, is not the focus of our analysis. Rather, the focus is on the true gambler, who takes delight in the rise and fall of fortune and who seeks out precisely those games in which no skill or calculation provides any advantage; for the preference is for sheer, wanton luck. This figure is not solely a game player but also one who dares to venture into danger and challenge, seeking the thrill of huge excitement, scorning caution, running those risks with high stakes and perilous adventure. There is, perhaps, some of the gambler and adventurer in all of us, though the more stolid influences of prudence and security may dampen the fervor; but even so, the lure of rash daring appeals to us, even if only from a safe and vicarious distance.

But why? To the cautious it may seem utterly foolish, even wicked. Why risk what is valuable on what cannot be controlled? A safe investment is not only more secure but also less alarming. Are not the adventurers and gamblers mere wantons who have nothing to offer thoughtful and rational people? Indeed, is not the very meaning of *gambler* one who has no respect for reason or control?

Yet we can give reasons for both gambling and daring. One does not gamble merely to make money, not even to make a great deal of money in an effortless way and in a short time. There are those who gamble moderately who seem to delight in the gamble itself, and not so much in the wealth lost or gained. How are we to make sense of this? Mark Twain points out, through his amiable urchin Huckleberry Finn, that we take more delight in the dollar we find on the ground than in the dollar we earn as our wage. And Huckleberry is a font of American wisdom, eternally young as he is. Why does Huck Finn say this?

We enjoy the found dollar more than the earned precisely because, in not having to labor for it, we celebrate its sheer bestowal. It is the recognition that who one is matters, and not merely what one does. Not knowing why we are smiled on by fortune intensifies this sense of the autonomy of our existential worth. We may appreciate a gift, too, bestowed on us by a doting relative, but then we owe gratitude and thanks and are beholden to the benefactor. But sheer fortuity makes no such demands. We may thank our lucky stars rather than Aunt Polly, but these stars are easier to thank because we do not know them and because there is no obligation to thank at all. Whether it is Tom Sawyer's Aunt Polly or the Christian God who bestows gifts, the need to thank may qualify the elation in receiving. But the sheer, wanton unintelligibility of our lucky find is not so burdened. No elation is as pure as unthanked, unearned, even undeserved elation that just pops up, unaccounted for, and favors *us*.

It is the *us* that matters to the philosopher. What is earned by labor is ours by right and depends on what we do and on contract; what is given by another depends on who we are in relation to the benefactor. Hence a gift is existentially more revealing than a wage. But what is found by sheer luck has no prior conditions or institutionalization, and this leaves us completely unadorned. We may be respected by the employer who pays our wage, we may be beloved by our Aunt Polly who gives us gifts, but we are ourselves when we find the dollar on the ground. The elation comes from the purest sense of our simple *being*, undetermined by any relationships.

It is this pure elation, which owes no thanks, no labor, no prior relationship, that is sought in gambling. It is also sought in daring, which is always a kind of gamble. There seems to be something worthwhile in daring or gambling, and this turns out to be the worth of our existence as such. The luck can be good or bad, the adventure harmful or innocent, but in any case what is important is the isolation of our own existence from any other considerations or conditions. Just to be aware of this autonomous meaning can be exhilarating, and when intensified it brings the elation that is the motivation for gambling.

What is important here, however, is not the motivation but the meaning. The gambler may indeed be motivated by a multitude of different reasons and causes, but what renders him intelligible is the celebration of his existence *as* autonomous from what he does and from those to whom he belongs and even from those by whom he is loved. He earns nothing, deserves nothing, owes nothing, is burdened by no obligation to repay or even to thank: he just *is himself* and that *being* who he is somehow is celebrated by the gambler's delight in the rawest of fortuity. Thus, rather than an impediment to thought, when philosophically examined the gambler provides a profound resource for a meaningful response to the fundamental question "why me?"

Nevertheless these reflections are disturbing. At the very least they seem to support indolence, lethargy, and aristocratic idleness. The importance of diligence, honor, hard work, and self-respect seems threatened by this praise of the arbitrary and the fickle. Were these analyses to be interpreted as somehow deprecating these virtues, the analysis would indeed be suspect. But no such depreciation is warranted. This is a philosophical inquiry, not moral instruction. The fact that there may be veridical value in the analysis of luck in no way implies the proscription that one ought to abandon the virtues of diligence and responsibility or even that one ought to take up moderate gambling. There is no 'ought' implied at all.

There is, nevertheless, much that is philosophically disturbing about these reflections, for they seem to suggest that knowledge and control in no way exhaust the range of intelligibility, that 'not to know something' is somehow more intelligible than to know it, and that 'not to control' something is somehow, in some circumstances, more *thinkable* than to control something. These suggestions are indeed intended by the reflections on the gambler, and it should be noted that they fly in the face of certain traditions that equate 'rational' with 'ordered' and 'thinkable' with 'knowable'. There may be sound, ethical prohibitions against gambling, but the philosophical analysis of its presuppositions is even more dangerous. Can this praise of the arbitrary be rendered *thinkable*? If 'to think' means to be able to succeed in approaching truth, and to provide some authority and law-likeness to our consciousness, then the answer must be yes. We not only can think about luck successfully—that is, penetrating with authority to the depths of truth—it turns out we *must* do so if we are to make coherent sense of our own existence. The gambler must be understood not only in terms of the delight he takes in feeling favored by fate but also in terms of what justifies or grounds such feelings. It is not merely how the gambler feels—for that could be perverse—but also why what the gambler feels is a legitimate source of thinking and elation. If the gambler takes delight in fortune, then fortune must mean something; if the delight is warranted, then the meaning is not dependent on a perverse misprizing but is grounded in reality.

Because we are extracting such important notions from it, the gamble must be precisely understood. One who knows perfectly well from past losses that continued gambling will most likely cost more than is gained may nevertheless refuse to surrender this activity simply because of what gambling reveals. It is tempting to believe that the gambler continues to wager costly sums because of a conviction that tomorrow will produce a bonanza, or that one gambles because of the accompanying delights of partnership with fellow gamblers or the atmosphere at the casinos. Perhaps these secondary considerations do indeed account for the continuing gambling of some wagerers, but these ulterior motives need not discredit the essential insight. It is possible to gamble just because to do so celebrates our independence from such calculations as prudence, sobriety, and thrift. Rather like one who takes pleasure in submitting to a lover's wants, the true gambler may actually take delight in being used or even abused by the randomness of fortune. The argument here is that such submission is not always perverse but indeed is supported by philosophical analysis. Unless we are capable of affirming our fate we are self-deceived. The gambler who affirms the sheer lack of knowledge, determination, and control is delighting in the manifestation of this truth. The true gambler, in other words, gambles not in order to win but simply to gamble, and thus accepts equally both good and bad luck, though preferring the former.

This reveals the deeper question. Am I required, by dint of reason and the reverence for truth, to claim that a world completely governed, controllable, and predictable is more thinkable and coherent, and hence preferable, to a world in which fate can be affirmed? When the question is put in such bold and direct terms, it would seem as if the former were indeed more coherent. But this must now be examined more closely.

What would an entirely unfated world be like? In such a world I would receive only the amount of happiness I deserve and would be visited only by the pain that I have earned. It would be an entirely just world. A world governed solely by morality and justice could permit of no forgiveness, since to forgive is to forfeit the grim necessity of punishment deserved. Nor could there be any grace; that is, benefits could not be given or received unless deserved. Although such a world may appear harsh, perhaps even grim, it is not inconceivable and, given the wanton abuse of privilege, may still be preferable. It is impossible of course to imagine such a world with only *desirable* bestowals, because even they are unearned; and if anyone is favored beyond their desert, even if it were to make everyone in the world happier, it would no longer be an unfated world. But is such a world coherent?

In such a world I receive only what I deserve. But I do not *deserve* to be born. I have not *earned* my existence. Hence, in such a world, I and all who have not earned or do not deserve existence would not *be*. In such a world, only those whose existence is inherently worthwhile could exist. Only a god could exist. It would be a world peopled only by necessary beings.

In such a world, thinking could not occur, for thinking is what finite beings must do in the absence of divine intuition, and so such a world is harsh, grim, graceless, bereft of finite humanity, and unthinkable, though not logically impossible. Precisely because human frailty cannot abide an absolutely just world and human finitude cannot grasp an absolutely knowable world, in celebrating the reality of our frailty, which needs forgiveness, and our finite understanding, which needs wonder, we must make room for fate.

This must be emphasized: the argument insists that we must make room not only for *ignorance* but also for *fate*. This is so because I cannot be said to have earned or deserved my existence. I am not merely *ignorant* of the forces that brought me, in all my privacy and peculiarity, into the world; I am rather *certain* that my own existence is unearned and undeserved. The biological laws that govern my conception, gestation, and birth explain not *me* but every living person equally, and hence cannot be used to explain the *worth* of my *unique* existence. Of course, one could deny both my worth and uniqueness and claim that in this perfectly unfated world I exist *merely* as a product of necessary, biological laws that explain everyone equally well but no *one* at all. And that, of course, is what the argument is all about. It is why we gamble. A world without fate explains everything *except* that we matter, uniquely. The gambler, in celebrating the sheer arbitrariness of his luck, is affirming the possibility that he *matters*.

Or rather, to be more precise, the gambler gambles because he is motivated by the *delight* in rejecting a purely governed universe. He delights in this without knowing exactly what it is. It is the philosopher who recognizes the importance of the gambler, because of what it *means* to be a gambler. We need not attribute philosophical sophistication to all who gamble. Again, we are speaking of meaning, not motivation.

But is it not perverse to take delight in losing? This is a troubling notion, but it need not be a distracting one. Certainly it is possible to enjoy a game without winning it, but whether one enjoys *losing* is irrelevant if the pleasure in playing is greater than that of either winning or losing. It may even be possible to take nonperverse pleasure in losing if such loss supports a sense of triumph over what is regulated and controlled.

But a certain reluctance to accept this line of existential argumentation requires deeper probing. Surely, the critic would say, the gambler deals not with fate but merely with chance, and chance, when pressed, turns out to be nothing but ignorance. We say, for example, that a flipped coin lands heads up by chance. What we mean is that the factors involved are so complex that we, given our limitations, cannot know them. If I knew exactly how much pressure to apply on my thumb or if I knew exactly all the other variables such as air currents in the room and the physical laws involved in spinning coins, I would indeed know exactly when the coin would turn up heads. It is because all who participate in the coin toss are equally ignorant of these factors that we rely on the coin toss to determine the winner. The same can be said for cards and roulette wheels. Certainly if x amount of energy under conditions y and z produced a coin landing heads up one time it would produce heads up coins every time. To deny this would deny the laws of physics.

This critique is warranted. But again the point must be made: no one is denying that physical events are determined by unalterable and ultimately determinable laws. It also is true that it is the mere ignorance of all the variables that allows us to consider the coin toss a result of chance. What is denied, however, is that the determination of physical laws is all that constitutes the realm of the *thinkable*; and it is also denied that the actual occurrence of these events operating under such laws alone constitutes reality and meaning. To believe in chance, or fate, is not to assert gaps in nature. It is merely to deny that thinking, reality, and meaning are restricted to such rule-governed events. For *what* I am may be determined by physical laws, but *who* I am is not; and what it *means* for me to exist most definitely is not.

The gambler who loses the coin toss is not questioning the unknown (but knowable) laws of physics and the conditions that brought about the coin landing the way it did. Rather he questions what it *means* for him to have been defeated in this instance by factors over which he has no control. The argument is not whether the conditions and physical laws could have been otherwise; the question is whether it is more rational to trust in chance than not to trust in chance. The gambler takes delight in trusting in chance partly because in doing so he repudiates a preference for a world in which the only rational way of thinking is to assume the unpalatable world described above, wherein rules, whether scientific, moral, or metaphysical, are the only resources for thinking and truth.

Nevertheless, the critique has pointed to a vulnerable spot in the analysis. Chance is not fate. It seems to stretch the word to say that a gambler relies on fate; surely it is more precise to say he relies on chance. Indeed, a nongambler may have a greater sense of fate than a gambler. We might argue that it is one's fate *to be* a gambler and that in gambling one relies on chance. Above all, our understanding of fate can never be found in the analysis of chance events such as the tossing of a coin.

Yet, though fate is not simply chance, it cannot be denied that chance plays an important role in our understanding of fate. To the uncontrolled, even if through mere ignorance, chance plays a fundamental role in how we think about ourselves and our stories. This examination of chance is meant not merely to show that fate and chance are different but also to show that chance opens a fascinating wedge into the problem of fate. What this reflection on chance has done is to fine-tune the range and method of the inquiry. The approach to fate cannot be realized merely by the study of random events, by ignorance of the physical laws or conditions, and certainly not by appealing to some mysterious causal agency that somehow escapes the law-likeness of our scientific principles. On the more positive side, the brief consideration of what a world without fate would be like has helped us focus on the kinds of responses we are seeking. It may seem paradoxical in the extreme to say that fate, which by definition cannot be explained causally or morally, is thinkable, indeed necessary, if we are to penetrate to the depth of truth about the meaning of existence. But paradoxes are not contradictions, and in this case the clearer the paradox is made, that is, the more we insist it *is* a paradox, the greater our chances of deepening our understanding.

The protest that the gambler's reliance on chance is not the same as the gambler's fate appeals to us because we seem to want to say that chance determines the gambler's winning or losing, but it is his *fate* that determines he is a gambler at all.

Fate characterizes in part *who* the gambler is, chance characterizes what the gambler *does*. To be sure, what one does is not entirely irrelevant to who one is; and thus chance is not entirely bereft of any significance for the inquiry into fate. In order to develop a fuller picture of the gambler's fate we would have to tell his story; we would have to make sense of those narrative and dramatic forces that mold his character in such a way as to delight in this risky rejection of order and in his preference for taking games seriously. But this would be to concern ourselves with the next chapter, in which the telling of stories is examined. Before proceeding to the historian, however, the gambler should be examined further.

■   ■   ■

The gambler plays games seriously. There is a gentle paradox even here, for one usually associates games with the unserious. We must eat and sleep and provide for our safety and health, but we do not have to play. Leisure is opposed to work just as luxury is opposed to necessity. The gambler seems to take perverse pleasure in upsetting these values, ranking leisure above work, for, again, the delights of leisure are unearned, the wages of labor are deserved. The gambler, then, remains somewhat opaque to us until and unless we are willing to probe into the importance of games. Fateful events strike the prudent and the gamester alike, but it is only the player who celebrates the fickleness of fortune, and it is the celebration that reveals how we think about these random favors or misfortunes. And so we must ask, what does it mean to play?

To say we play because it gives pleasure may be true but misses the point. We want to know *why* we enjoy playing, and to answer this without recourse to circularity in explanation requires that play be understood independently of the pleasure it brings. After all, some kinds of labor can also bring pleasure, and some kinds of play may bring considerable pain and effort. We distinguish leisure from labor in terms of their achievement: labor is what brings about what is earned, leisure brings nothing except perhaps a celebration of who we are. But this distinction, so described, is not a source of enlightenment but further puzzlement. There is no denying that the labor-leisure distinction is itself a great philosophical problem at least as old as Plato, and it is the purpose of this chapter not to resolve all the difficulties but merely to appeal to it as a source of understanding the gambler as one who plays.

When Cassuis asks Brutus if he will see "the running of the course," he demurs, saying:

> I am not gamesome: I do lack some part of that quick spirit that is in Antony.
>
> *Julius Caesar*, I, 2

In one brush-stroke, Shakespeare paints a clear picture of the difference between the two heroes. Brutus is stolid, reliable, honorable, constant, and thoroughly Roman. Antony is "gamesome," beloved by Caesar, favored, fleet of foot, attractive, and, in *this* play, victorious. Antony's gamesomeness will eventually bring him down as well in the later Roman tragedy shared with the wondrous Cleopatra; but in *Julius Caesar* it is Brutus's character that weaves his fated doom. How are we to understand this? Brutus, deeply patriotic, loves the Republic

of Rome and is so loyal to this institution that he is willing to
destroy her enemy even if it is Caesar himself, whom Brutus
loves as a friend. Antony loves Caesar, too, both as a man and
as one who embodies greatness. Though Antony also loves
Rome, he could not betray his beloved friend to save her re-
publican government. It is he who describes the fallen Brutus
as "the noblest Roman of them all." Which figure does Shakespeare want us to prefer? Are we to love our friends above
our nations? Are we to serve greatness rather than what is
right? Or is the greatness of a nation more important than the
greatness of a single man? Shakespeare's genius far surpasses
these questions: his is not a moral lesson preferring the one
over the other. The play is a tragedy because both Brutus and
Antony have legitimate characters and defensible causes. We
can no more argue for Brutus over Antony than we can argue
for Antigone over Creon.

But Antony is "gamesome" and Brutus is not. *This* tells us
much, perhaps all we need to know. This lack of playfulness
tends to make Brutus somehow incapable of seeing the illus-
trious glamour of a would-be Roman king. For Brutus, it is
simply not *Roman* to have a Roman king; for Romans are
ruled by law and reason, not men, no matter how great or
glorious. Antony's playfulness allows him to transcend the Roman law, and his eye is quick to appreciate the glamour a
majestic presence would bring to the overly coddled citizenry
of the world's then greatest nation. Antony is far more contemptuous of the Roman rabble than is Brutus, and, in the
two great oratorical speeches to the crowds in act III, it is
Antony's contemptuous manipulation of them that turns them
against their true defender, Brutus, who spoke to them as
equals, under the Roman law. But Antony's success seems to
prove his point: the rabble is but rabble, and Rome's true
greatness needs a great, imperious ruler. The Republic stands
for what is good and right, but Caesar offers greatness.

The outwitted but noble Brutus would protest: it is Rome that is truly great, not a Caesar. In his speech to the crowd, Brutus asks if any of them would prefer to be slaves. Antony, in *his* speech to the crowd, asks if any of them are not men, and hence would not weep. Brutus appeals to their honor and their reason, Antony to their hearts and their spirit. Must we choose between them?

The gamesome Antony is spirited, the stolid Brutus is honorable. The tension simply cannot be relieved: we need and want them both. We do not want to be slaves, and so we honor Brutus; we do not want to be spiritless, and so we honor Antony. As we shall see in a subsequent chapter, such tension is the essence of tragedy. But here we reflect on the play for what it reveals about the *gamesome*. And what *does* it reveal?

Though the gambler, as gamesome, is appreciated, he is also seen as imprudent; he is beloved, perhaps, like a rakish bachelor uncle whose visits are exciting but slightly wicked. We have seen that a world with no chance or fate is unthinkable; but a world of only chance and no order is unlivable. And at the very least this shows us that games, and the ultimate life of leisure they represent, are of value *only* if they are countered by the more prudential realms of labor and honor. In witnessing Shakespeare's play we are highly distressed as Brutus reluctantly joins the scabrous Cassius and the conspiracy to kill the radiant Caesar; but we are even more overwhelmed by the casual indifference of Antony after he joins up with the other two triumvirs, proscribing death to so many with a wave of the hand. "He shall not live; look, with a spot I damn him" (IV, 1). The rule of terror is not a game, though it is the gamesome and not the honorable that inevitably employ it as policy. Thus, though Antony may be more beloved and even loving, his rakish spirit of play is far more deadly when unchecked.

To play is therefore admirable as a check against the dour, but it cannot suffice to provide us with all we need. Leisure has long been praised as the spiritual force that moves a people to greatness. The Greeks were known for their spirit of play, and all art and culture are achieved only in leisure. Christ makes the same point that Plato makes when he compares his apostles to the useless but beautiful flowers: "Consider the lilies of the field, how they grow; they toil not, neither do they spin. And yet I say unto you, that even Solomon in all his glory was not arrayed like one of these" (Matthew 6:28–29). But we do not feed on lilies.

Antony may be gamesome, but it is Roman law and not Roman games that makes the city on the Tiber wonderful. The gambler as gamesome is precious to us, as are the lilies, only because there is already a steadiness and reliability in what is dependable and constant. To the extent to which the gamble reflects on our understanding of fate, the parallel is clear. Fate is meaningful, in both its drastic and favoring senses, only when it is set against the more fundamental, if less exciting, constancy of order and reason. (On the deepest level the spirit of Brutus and that of Antony are less antithetic than complementary, though to say this now is perhaps preemptive.)

■　　■　　■

The woman, tired, haggard, much younger than she looked, pinched with penury and drained of resilience, wearily extracted the wrinkled dollar bill from her cracked plastic purse and asked the clerk for a lottery ticket.

"You could save this dollar, you know. Your youngest child needs milk."

"I know," she said. "But I buy one, just one, every two weeks."

"Expect you'll win a million, do you?"

She shook her head, sadly. "Don't expect so, really."

"But you can hope, I guess."

"No. Hoping . . . hurts. You know."

"But why . . . then?"

A distant, ephermeral smile, more in her eyes than on her lips, seemed to lighten her just for a moment. She picked up the ticket and put it in her purse. "With this, honey, I can dream."

Some gamblers expect to win, some hope to win; others are content to dream. That we dream at all, in the sense of the woman with the lottery ticket, is remarkable in itself. Chance, opened by this gambler, makes possible the possible; it makes the dream of another world more than sheer illusion. She knows the odds against her are astronomical, but that firm, bright-colored cardboard in her purse is her assurance that her dream of what is not the case and most probably will never be the case is nevertheless within the realm of chance. The player dreams, and because of this the world is wider than all the sorrows and all the suffering that we know. It may not even be hope, which can be a cruel noise that awakens the slumbering discontent; the dream, which needs merely to be anchored by chance too thin for hope, is enough. It is the gift of the 'ungoverned'.

■   ■   ■

What has this cursory examination of the gambler revealed? Seven items can be enumerated.

1. 'Chance' is not the same as 'fate'.
2. Chance and fate are bestowals that do not entail an indebtedness, and hence are elations without the demand for gratitude, so that thanking is itself bestowed.
3. The 'ungoverned'—that which is unpredictable and beyond our control—can be affirmed.

4. What is ungoverned is not the natural world or even the moral world but the realm of meaning.
5. Play (leisure) is a source of greatness (meaning).
6. Leisure presupposes the governed or ordered.
7. Gambling opens up dreams.

These seven points will be reconsidered in greater detail after the reflection on the remaining three figures. The first of these points, that chance is not fate, reminds us that when we speak of the fate of a gambler we must tell his story. And so we turn to the two figures who do tell stories.

3
. . .

THE HISTORIAN
Fate as Destiny

HISTORICAL DESTINY

Why do we 'do' history? By 'doing' history as opposed to 'making' it, I mean reading it, writing it, studying it, building monuments, making holidays to commemorate events, and searching for our origins and meanings in the sagas of our ancestors. Why *do* these things at all? There are a few who doubt the wisdom of history altogether, though probably none surpass the contempt ladled out on it by Henry Ford's remark that "history is more or less bunk."

Yet Ford's philistine remark may be true; there is at least a ring of honesty about it. Far more dubious are those who honor it with faint or even deceitful praise. George Santayana, in *The Life of Reason,* writes famously that "those who cannot remember the past are doomed to repeat it." But this suggests we study history only to avoid the pitfalls of human folly; history is merely a prudential resource for success. But the truth, much less the value, of this is highly suspect. It is just as often the case that overemphasis on history brings about disaster. Witness the historical French in their struggles with the innovative Germans. In defeat in 1870 at Sedan they learned that an aggressive offense was the key to victory in war, that is, until 1914, when they ran into a new weapon in the German ranks, the machine gun. From *this* defeat they learned the wisdom of defense, built the Maginot line, and were defeated by an even newer weapon—the tank. The wisdom of the past became the folly of the old. But even if there *are* things in history from which we can learn how to be prudent—and surely there are many—this seems to make history a mere filing cabinet of usable warnings against making mistakes, some of which are entirely bankrupt by the newer and bolder achievements of the nonhistorical attitude—like that of Henry Ford. There was no historical precedent for horseless carriages, and Ford was quite right in debunking this as a reason not to build them.

And who is so wise as to know what history teaches anyway? For every major historical event there are twenty conflicting interpretations as to what it means and what lessons it provides. Learning from history is as risky as learning from the ancient oracles: both speak in riddles. Because speculation on the future may provide equal or superior prudential wisdom to the study of the past and because the past remains shrouded by conflicting interpretation, Santayana's defense of it seems shallow indeed.

And yet we still do history, and properly so. It is neither bunk nor a study guide for success. It is rather something that has intrinsic worth and not mere extrinsic value. We *do* history because we *are* historical; it is built into our deepest natures that our stories and our origins matter. But *why* should this be the case? Why is the study of past events any more important or revealing than the study of present events? Or is history even to be understood as the study of past events?

Let us imagine a perfect chronicler of all that happens. With the wondrous development of technology, such a device is not totally beyond our grasp. An orbiting satellite could televise everything that happens and store it for convenient retrieval at the demand of a viewer. With this device, one could recall, by means of videotape, any moment or event that takes place—the perfect, error-free chronicle that could replace all archives, notes, history books and referats that are now used by historians to do their job. Would the viewing of such a videotape constitute 'doing' history? If history is the chronicle of past events, such a device would make the writing of history books irrelevant and passé. Its memory banks would *be* history.

And yet we sense that this perfect chronicler would not be history at all. Why? At the very least it would seem that one would need a further resource that would tell us which events to look at, which were important and which trivial. It would be difficult to imagine a machine that could make judgments of this sort, sifting out ordinary, everyday affairs and focusing on those that have great significance. There must have been a Roman farmer somewhere who broke his plow the day Caesar crossed the Rubicon; why is the farmer less significant than Caesar? And even if it were possible to develop a procedure to distinguish the significant from the insignificant, however wildly improbable that seems, would this chronicle of the major events even yet provide us with a *historical* sense? The intuition that it would not is not enough. We need to understand *why* it would not. But what is history if it is not the perfect chronicle?

The chronicle of events, even if perfectly recorded, is not history because such recall in and of itself does not tell a story. In both French and German, the word for history is the same as the word for story, '*l'histoire*' and '*Geschichte*'. But history is not just any story; indeed it is not merely any *true* story. History is *our* story, and its unfolding may reveal more about our being in time than any other activity. For in the unfolding of history, if the story is well told, a vague but irresistible sense of our destiny as a people cannot entirely be avoided. As a consequence, something profound about our essential nature is uncovered: we are beings of destiny. What this means exactly and how we are to think about it may not be settled, but *that* an essential characteristic of our species is destiny can be denied only if the telling of our story is itself a fantasy.

We should perhaps pause to note that many historians of differing stripes boldly assert this unfolding destiny in their interpretations. A Marxist interprets all of human history as a dialectic toward the development of a social synthesis; some Christians see the unfolding of events as preparing for the day of judgment. Doomsayers see us racing toward oblivion; social evolutionists see us crawling toward ever better worlds; eastern mystics see the turning of the great wheel, repeating cycles forever. On less cosmic scales, the eighteenth-century historian sees the unfolding of the British Constitution; Nazis read it as the inevitable triumph of one race over another; some now read history as the struggle of an oppressed gender against the oppressor sex. We are going to be damned or saved, redeemed, or conquered by the insects, but there can be no doubt we are *going* one way or other; up or down, we are headed somewhere. If not, why tell the story at all?

And even if an author pretends only to put down the facts, and hence qualifies as a 'scientist', the reader will provide his own sense of destiny. It matters not at all that there are so many contenders telling us what this destiny is and that all contradict one another; it would indeed be odd if these disputes did not occur, for the story is wondrous and complex, the indicators multiple and confused, the issue of supreme urgency and concern; but alas our faculties are extremely limited. The writers and readers of history are, after all, a part of history as well, and any attempt to deny this or even circumvent it by distortion merely obfuscates even more. But that there is the thrust of destiny inevitably woven into the fabric of our story can be denied only when we stop telling the story altogether: it is why the story is told.

We do not need to have this destiny expressed or grounded in an ideology or religion; indeed we may not have even the vaguest sense of what it might be. But that is one of the reasons we read the histories and contemplate the monuments: to find out what this destiny is, or at least to sensitize ourselves to its subtle message. That there is such a message, that all these stories and tributes and public memories show us the role we play in the unfolding of a truth that surpasses our planning, control, and full comprehension, is irresistible. For this is what we mean by destiny, that we as a people are going someplace, that as a people our existential meaning can be thought about, supported, and even revered, but never mastered. We do not make it happen; it makes us who we are. There is no denial of personal freedom in such claims; rather freedom itself is rendered intelligible only because in our brief, allotted journey through our age, we are already thinkable, we already matter, we are already meaningful. Unless we already mattered, nothing we do could be free; our desires and our conditions would be our masters.

And so, like chance for the gambler, destiny for the historian is an appeal to the ungoverned and uncontrolled that nevertheless can be affirmed and even, perhaps, be somewhat understood. It is closer to fate than chance, but destiny is still only a step—a closer step—to the understanding of fate. Unlike chance, destiny is available to us in far more intimate ways. Chance on the one hand always seems a distant, random, and cosmic force, indifferent to our character; destiny on the other hand is an existential reality, that part of who we are beyond our control; it beckons us to struggle and to trek the distance.

What concrete indication is there that such a notion as historical destiny is anything more than an illusion that props up dubious ideologies? An example of how the reading of an actual, historical account entails something like a sense of destiny may help the analysis. Consider what happens, for example, when we read of the social and political events that led to the outbreak of war in 1914. In some accounts we seem to sense an irresistible drift toward conflict. It seems as if the war were bound to happen, that even had the assassins at Sarajevo failed to kill the Archduke, some other spark, trivial or earth-shaking, sooner or later would have ignited one among the ample fuses that carried the flash of heat to the powder keg. It is hard to escape feeling this sentiment. The hounds of war were baying and hungry and the leashes that held them back were pitiful in their weakness. It is easy to believe, in reading of these tragic times, that there was a force at work that simply could not have been derailed from its journey toward Armageddon. War, in 1914, was determined. Such readings seem to imply that we simply are not free in such cases.

And yet one can read the very same texts and sense an entirely opposite feeling: if only the driver of the Archduke's car had not turned down Franz-Joseph street; if only the Kaiser had been informed of what the Austrians were up to; if only Tsar Nicholas had acted more decisively sooner; or, if that is too much to expect, if only he had hesitated just a few more days to sign the mobilization papers. As Churchill wrote, the terrible ifs accumulate. But if this second impression is the truer one, if some tiny alteration of incidence would have actually avoided the war, are we really in a superior position? The implication of this second view is that the sheerest chance can unravel civilization. Is the Leviathan of history captive of these Lilliputian trivialities? The consequences of a petty act or event that in itself seems scarcely worth the ink to write it down are so titanic we cannot believe the one explains the other. History is a mere chronicle of meaningless and insignificant occurrences that have results far in excess of their power to explain. If we accept the first reading, we forfeit our freedom and responsibility to the power of the inevitable; but if we accept the second, we forfeit all to the vagaries of the insignificant. Which is the greater submission? If we cannot ask which makes more sense, we might at least ask which is less shameful. In his preface to *The Course of Empire*, Bernard de Voto writes, "History abhors determinism but cannot tolerate chance."

The third impression one might take from the reading of these dreadful days is that of blame. History is an indictment of the race. Responsibility and guilt explain all, and the blood of millions is on the hands of the wicked few. Perhaps this is true; certainly there is some truth in it. But the guilt of a misguided fanatic such as Gavrilo Princip, a weak-willed tsar, a blustery kaiser with a shrunken hand, is no more illuminating of the great story than are appeals to wretched misfortunes. To explain the war by blaming the Austrian, French, German, Russian, and Serbian ministers and kings is to deny the very power of the story that seems to unite the disparate factions into a coherent line. Blame trivializes the blamer. There were villains in the story, and their responsibility and guilt cannot, or should not, be denied. But that is just the point: their wickedness is *in* the story; it is the story that accuses and indicts. But so are the accidents and misfortunes in the story. And so, too, are those elements that make us feel the inevitable drift toward doom; they, too, are *in* the story. And we need them all: the tiny misfortunes we cannot control, the responsibility and guilt we can and should control, the thrust of the narrative that knits the errant threads into whole cloth. They all are parts of a story.

And this is what suggests a transcendent explanation, for how are we to understand the vast grid of countless coincidence and the trifles of misfortune, the shame and the necessity? How do we weave the warp of guilt with the woof of chance? Merely to appeal to sheer coincidence and the responsibilities of the unworthy, when the story of mortal success is at stake, is to confess that the telling of it makes no sense.

But is this not to admit that destiny, if it is to be a meaningful notion, is not in what really happens but simply in the telling of it? And is this not a confession that destiny is but a perspective, a subjective bias, of storytellers to make our unpalatable misery easier to swallow? If the destiny of a people is discovered only in the telling of a story, then perhaps the telling is at fault.

But is it a *fault*? To be sure, destiny is revealed only in the telling of our story, not in the events themselves and not even in the moral responsibility of the agents. But this does not demean its worth, for what is told, our story, is a resource of truth. This last claim is perhaps remarkable and certainly cannot remain unsupported and uncriticized. But if it is so that the telling of our story is an instance of truth, then we must consider deeply two questions: What is a story? And whose story is it? Only by the analysis of these two questions can we hope to gain purchase of the more elusive, but more important, notion of destiny.

THE STORY

What, then, is a story? We are told by those who have thought about such things that stories have a beginning, middle, and end; that they have three constituents: character, plot, and theme; that there are various purposes to a story: to instruct, entertain, inspire, persuade, improve, and elevate or depreciate the soul, among others. Stories are either fact or fiction, and in their greatest form they occur in the arts of the novel, short story, epic, comedy, tragedy, history, film, video, and opera. Brief stories are even used to market manufactured goods on the public media. We are therefore familiar with stories as they surround us in our daily lives, and, whether fact or fictive, we seem to know in advance the form and structure of a story almost as instinctively as we know that events have causes or that caution is safer than trust.

This may, however, be far more than familiarity. Perhaps the form of a story lies a priori in our consciousness the way

Kant claims the structures of causality and time do; perhaps the structure of the story is a category, not of sensed experience as it is for Kant but of existential meaning. If this is so, then we do not learn about the past and then tell a story; rather we first (a priori) already know the form of a story and through this structure learn about the past. And furthermore, if this is true, it is not memory that makes stories possible but the telling of stories that gives meaning to memory.

What is the (possibly) a priori structure of the story? It is at the very least the priority of the interconnectedness of events that makes the events possible. When the child hears the opening "once upon a time," he knows immediately that what follows is significant in terms of what precedes; that the ensuing events are meaningful only because of the power that a story has to unite them as things worthy of attention. The listener hears in the story the past pregnant with the present and the present promising the future. It is not the past that makes the story possible but the story that makes the past possible. Stories are *characters plotted on a theme*, and unless this is understood prior to the actual unfolding there is no way the various occurrences or adventures can congeal into a meaningful discourse.

If this is true, it is not character, plot, and theme that make up stories but stories that allow for character, plot, and theme; the same reversal can be said of the beginning, middle, and end. We are beings whose very intelligibility depends upon the coherence of this narrative structure; perhaps we might even say we *are* our stories. We often equate 'my life' with 'my story', suggesting an identity or at least isomorphism of meanings between the two terms. My life is my story; perhaps, since I, too, have a beginning, a middle, and an end, as stories do, to be is simply to be unfolded. Certainly my own persisting through a period of time is reflective of how stories are told, and this obvious truth may yield the more profound one: we are intelligible *only* as stories.

Some observations may be made about stories that, when considered with due reflection, may illuminate their priority as a way of thinking. In some intelligence tests, the subject is given a random collection of various cartoon drawings and is asked to arrange them in a story, the way the panels of a comic strip represent succeeding moments in the unfolding of the narrative. The subject is expected not to have known the story, which is usually minimalist and void of entertainment, but rather to be able to arrange the panels in a narratively coherent pattern. This device assumes that a mark of intelligence is the capacity to see separate events interconnectedly; or perhaps more importantly it shows that the inability to structure these panels in narrative coherence is a deficiency in human understanding. To be able to arrange the panels properly indicates we have a prior inclination to think in terms of narrative coherence.

A second observation may now be made. Nathaniel Hawthorne, in a brilliant stroke, titled the collection of some of his stories *Twice-Told Tales*. The suggestion implied in the title is, of course, that these stories are worthy of repetition, that among the countless stories told throughout our history only a few deserve to be told over and over again. There is delight in the retelling. Most of us have our favorite stories that seem to become more satisfying the more they are told.

But what does this reveal? At the very least it shows that our appreciation of stories does not consist solely, or even mainly, in the discovery of what eventually happens. Stories do not tell us about events but rather show us what they mean, and hence their repetition can be enjoyed even more than their first encounter. Unlike causal explanations that produce knowledge, the narrative explanation reveals understanding.

Why does Shakespeare, for example, who is a master storyteller, have the chorus in *Romeo and Juliet* tell us in *advance* of the play what is going to happen? After we learn from these opening lines that the star-crossed lovers will take their lives, is there any reason for us even to stay in the theater? By spilling the beans before the first act, Shakespeare has taken all the suspense out of the play, ruining our chance to delight in the discovery of what happens.

Oddly, though also obviously, the suspense is not lessened but increased by this technique. Knowing the lovers are doomed in no way releases our suspense; instead it is amplified. Why? The reason is because the realm of the story is that not merely of providing information but also of showing us how to think and feel. Our fifth witnessing of a production of the play is more draining, more suspenseful, and more satisfying than our third or fourth (disregarding the quality of the performances). By clearing away all concern for what happens, Shakespeare directs our attention to the artistry by which he unfolds the story. The arts of dramaturgy and poetry are not eclipsed by mere anxiety for the outcome. If our worry throughout the drama centers on whether Romeo and Juliet will in fact make good their escape, we will then terminate our interest in the unfolding of the drama as soon as the curtain falls. But if we are not expected to concern ourselves with the resolution, then why do we watch the play? The answer is so obvious it is often overlooked. The very unfolding of the story itself is what grips us, not the outcome. In fact, by rendering the outcome irrelevant as a reason for watching the play, Shakespeare shows us that we celebrate the telling of a story just for the sake of the telling, not for the information we receive as to what actually happens.

The significance of this observation is of supreme importance. Stories do explain, but *what* they explain is different in kind from what is explained by scientific or causal explanations in nature. What we expect from a story is not the new information revealed by the outcome of events but the meaning, that is, thinkability, of being narrative-revealed creatures.

It is for this reason that the experts have divided the story into three distinct but interdependent elements: character, theme, and plot. In *Romeo and Juliet* the artistry of Shakespeare reveals to us almost endless richness in the characterization of the dramatis personae: we love the girlish delight of the Juliet in the first three acts, but then we admire the womanly maturity she develops in the fourth and fifth; we admire the boldness of the young Montague, but as we rewatch the play his vulnerabilities strike us as endearing as well. The *theme*, love and fate, is so aptly developed we seem never to tire of watching it unfold; and the tragic *plot* rarely fails to move us on the deepest level. To be sure, none of these elements can stand alone, but their importance shows us that the story is not merely in the service of what eventually happens at the end.

Indeed, the greatest stories surpass even the moral points that may justify the telling of an Aesop fable. Shakespeare often leaves us morally confused or, perhaps better, morally indifferent; for the themes and plots of greatly told stories are not reducible to mere moral instruction any more than they are ways to make sense of what happens in the world. This is not to deny that many stories do indeed have moral themes; it is merely to show that not all themes are moral ones, and perhaps the greatest are not.

If history, then, is a story, it too must have the three elements. The character of history is, of course, ourselves, either as members of this nation, this culture and religion, or even humanity itself. The theme is the meaningfulness of our existence; it is revealed in the triumphs and the failures of all the villains and the heroes that make up the cast.

But what is the plot? If history is a story it must have a plot; but plots apparently are realized only when the story comes to an end. Because history does not yet have an end, is it proper to identify it as a story at all? The plot of history is the subject of this chapter: it is our destiny. Stories are appreciated not only at their conclusion but also in their telling: that there will be an "end" is enough. It is precisely because we do not know the outcome that we understand the plot as a force that unifies the action into a narrative whole, and for our history this plot is destiny. The ends of fictive stories are not entirely unexpected or unknown. Indeed, if the story is extremely well told, the hearer or reader senses, perhaps vaguely but yet irresistibly, the nature of the impending conclusion. So, too, with actual histories of periods, peoples, or events, the conclusions are known when the stories are read. A well-told story of World War I can be read as pregnantly as a devised novel. What the good historian offers that distinguishes him from a chronicler is his power to evoke a narrative structure, and that means having a plot. A plot, after all, is simply making the end of the story follow meaningfully from the middle and the beginning; the historian does this, sometimes artfully, sometimes subtly, or sometimes with the heavy-handedness of ideological persuasion, to the extent that he evokes a sense of destiny.

That destiny is perforce something over which we exercise no persuasive control is neither unexpected nor undesirable. Any story that unfolds solely as the result of cunning, calculation, and will is not a history but a tribunal seeking judgment: censure or praise. A juror, listening to an account of a defendant's actions and culpability, is hearing not a history but an indictment. It may qualify as a story, as it too has a plot—the power of the telling that leads to judgment of guilt or innocence—but it is not a history since it lacks the element of destiny.

The argument is basically simple. History is a story, a chronicle is not. All stories have a plot. A plot unifies the various elements in such a way that the final result seems narratively contained in what precedes it; the final result must either be told or at least be implicit in the telling; the final result is not known in our history, though it may be known in historical accounts of completed epochs or events; and the plot of history is called destiny. When put in this way, historical destiny seems less fantastic than ideological accounts, but the problem remains: destiny (or the 'plot' of history) is dependent solely on the telling of a story and hence may be suspect. This problem, however, is by no means fatal to the argument; its menace is greatly lessened when we recognize that because history is the telling of a story with both theme and plot presupposed, its telling can still be true. History seeks truth in its telling, not in what the telling is *about*. What disturbs the critic is not that there must be a plot in any story nor the realization that history is a story; rather, the critic is disturbed that our understanding of destiny may have no testable justification. Perhaps, he may argue, there is a vague sense of destiny inevitable in history, but which view or which ideological account of what the destiny is cannot be decided by any rational means.

But this critique assumes that all historical stories are equally good or equally true, which they are not. There is a peculiar purpose to history when viewed philosophically: *to render intelligible our finite and temporary existence as characters in the drama of time.* Not all stories that purport to be historical do this equally well. The poor historian is not one who misleads us by telling what is false; rather, the poor historian is one who fails to make our temporal existence meaningful. Because in this endeavor one can note the difference between those who do it well and those who do it badly, the misology feared by the critique is misprized. It is precisely because we can distinguish good historians from bad ones that the criticism that all interpretations are merely subjective is thwarted. Furthermore, history is *judged* (as good or bad storytelling) not on the basis that events described happened or did not but on the telling itself. If the destiny of history is discoverable only in the telling and not in the truth or falsity of described events, and if history consists *in* the telling, but the telling can be *judged*, then the fear of a relativistic subjectivism is unwarranted.

But how are we to understand this 'telling'? A comparison of the historian with the architect may be helpful. We may enter buildings to get in out of the rain, or to get warm, or to do business, or to seek security, or to find a place for eating and sleeping. Or we can enter a building to discover, from the skill of the architect, what it means to dwell. The architect, through his art, reveals the truth about man the dweller. A well-designed building not only provides shelter but also accomplishes the possibility of dwelling, so that in the absence of designed buildings there is no dwelling at all. We do not first dwell and then hire architects to build buildings in order to dwell; rather architects first reveal, through their art, the meaning of dwelling, and in their buildings we dwell for the first time. Prior to architecture, we seek shelter, security, and privacy; after architecture, and because of it, we are dwellers. To enter a great cathedral is to learn what it means to worship; to enter a great university hall is to learn what it means to learn; to enter a great auditorium is to learn what it means to listen to music. These are all forms of dwelling, and such modalities do not preexist that which makes them possible. Hunger suffices to explain our eating, but only cuisine can explain our dining. By this analogy, purely purposive buildings do not succeed as architecture. But suppose one asks, what *is* dwelling other than seeking security and comfort? The answer is that you must look at a great building to find out. Philosophical reflections on what is provided by architecture may bring what is sensed to the level of thought, and indeed such thinking may deepen the architect's power to reveal; but no philosopher can reflect on the meaning of dwelling without first entering and submitting to what the building provides.

Does this render 'dwelling' an entirely subjective notion? Of course not. It merely shows that dwelling must await the architect to reveal its possibility. Not all buildings succeed equally well, but to one sensitized to such things the power of architecture to reveal the meaning of dwelling—and hence to awaken in us something important about who we are, namely, that we are dwellers—cannot be denied.

If this is true of the architect, how can we press the analogy to tell us about the historian, among whom we now must include the makers of monuments and the writers of cultural epics and historical dramas? The historian, by telling our story, changes who we are as surely as the architect changes us from shelter-users to dwellers. He does so by making our origins and our past matter. In this special philosophical sense, we *have* no past without the telling of it. In the purely natural sense, of course, I must be first a child before a youth and an adolescent before a man; but unless these prior stages can be understood *as* stages leading toward the fullness of maturity, they have no meaning whatsoever. The mind may project backward from a rock and imagine the volcanic explosion that put it on the hillside, but the rock has no history. As in the case of the architect, we do not first have a past and then hire a historian to tell us about it; rather, 'having a past' is possible only through the art of the storyteller. Hence, the historian is essential for self-understanding. Note that I do not claim that having ancestors does this, for the sheer fact of being in the chain of evolutionary predecessors is not enough: someone must tell the story if the chain is even to be realized.

Indeed, the telling of the story is more important than the accuracy of the account. The earliest storytellers were doubtless more fanciful than precise, more mythical than scientific, but as weavers of revealing tales they were masterful—or at least some of them were; and those peoples blessed with great tellers produce greater civilizations than those who lack them. The later concern for accuracy is due not to disdain for the power of myth but to the awesome realization that the unfolding story honors truth in its telling.

The architect, as noted earlier, literally changes the *reality* of who we are by replacing the shelter with the dwelling. So, too, the historian literally changes the *reality* of who we are by replacing the chronicle of past experience with the *inheritance* of a culture and a people. This inheritance fundamentally changes our very natures, because with it our collective memory now matters. The architect makes space matter, the historian makes time matter. The architect uses such elements as elevation, horizon, depth, nearness, and farness as well as massiveness and grace. The historian uses the characters, the themes, and the destiny of a people along with suspense, morals, and development. Thus destiny becomes available only through our history, and through it truth about who we are is made possible.

As we have seen in the analysis of the gambler, there are factors in our lives over which we have no control. When this fundamental trait of human existence is woven into a story that is both true and ours, it becomes destiny. But destiny, unlike chance, is not merely the realm of the unknown and ungoverned; it is also that which gives a peculiar direction to the unfolding story of a people. Just as a good architect will use the very massiveness and impenetrability of stone to reveal the foundational support of his building and hence the role that impenetrability plays in what *dwelling* means, so a historian will use the very impenetrability of a people's destiny to knit up the story's narrative weave and thereby expose impenetrability as inevitable in our narrative existence.

For the architect, walls are essential for the declaration of space; limits add grace to our spatiality. So, too, the opaque is essential for the historian; without the limits of our destiny, our temporality would be without surprise, suspense, or interest. A story told only with the elements of control and responsibility would be as ungracious as a building without walls. To be sure, the walls *enclose* and hence limit, but limit is the essence of dwelling. For the historian, destiny *discloses* by limiting our predictability and control, but without this disclosing limitation the story could not unfold any more than without walls the building could enclose. Stone walls are impenetrable, and so we have houses; people's destinies are impenetrable, and so we have history.

Thus history is the unfolding of our true story in which destiny provides the uncontrolled but thinkable plot that unites the disparate moments. But if *we* are the characters of this drama, who 'we' are must now be considered.

THE CHARACTERS

History unfolds our story and in the telling reveals our destiny. But who are 'we' whose story is unfolded? Is history only of a nation, told only by a native? Would world history, then, be impossible? Or would an entirely disinterested, objective telling by a foreigner of the English Civil War be impossible? To deny such things seems an exercise in utmost silliness, for surely there are non-English historians who write about the struggle between Charles Stuart and Oliver Cromwell; and perhaps not being English they provide a more objective account. With the shrinking of the global village it may seem unduly provincial to describe history as the unfolding of *a people's* destiny; indeed, our contemporary consciousness may prefer to see all history as the telling of humanity's story and a particular nation's history as merely a small part or chapter of the larger drama. Western thinkers, it would seem, should avail themselves of the stories of Japan and Africa no less so than the parochial tales of the smallest continent. By overcoming the provincialism and war-sponsoring nationalism in the telling of the widest story possible, that of the human race, deep racial and chauvinistic prejudice can at least be muted if not avoided. If this description is to be acceptable to the contemporary conventions, it must appear that by 'we' one must mean 'the human race', all of us.

There is honor and goodness in this sentiment, but its truth is less obvious. Perhaps there can be a world history, but only if there is first a local history. There are many peoples in the world, and each has its own destiny; and without destiny there can be no history. Is there a destiny to the entire human race? Possibly, but only as a result of the intertwining destinies, for in its original sense destiny is a characteristic only of peoples, and the human race is not a people. An individual can have a destiny only in the sense that he or she represents his or her culture, nation, or extended family. If destiny is found only in the unfolding of *our true story* and is hence not a metaphysical, cosmic *cause*, then differing peoples must have differing destinies, since to be a people is to have a unique story. In order to be a people, we must stand out from others, we must be heroic or villainous, or sometimes one and sometimes another; we must be able to be threatened, to rise and fall and rise again; we must confront the dread possibility of eclipse, the shame of failure, the giddy ecstasy of triumph. But triumphs are over others; failures are submissions to destinies of others, and because there are others with whom we interrelate, two questions arise. The first question is how we can retain our uniqueness in the commerce with others, the second is how we can amplify the range of our meaning by adopting and assimilating the influence of others.

Napoleon championed the destiny of France. But in doing so he also influenced the destiny of Europe. Italians, Belgians, Austrians, and Germans became involved in this French-dominated but surely European expansion of conquest, liberation, terrorism, and internationalism. For this reason a Dutch historian can write about the destiny of the French Revolution and the Napoleonic surge because the Dutch are to this extent French. Napoleon briefly made the French 'we' the European 'we'. And because of such things, there can obviously be a European destiny, and perhaps even a world destiny, but only in a derived sense. For a

destiny concerns *us,* and unless there are others that stand
out against *us,* the term has no meaning.

The idea that destiny presupposes a meaningful sense of
the term 'we' may be more difficult for our contemporary conventions than the idea of destiny itself. Ever since the
seventeenth-century Enlightenment, modern and contemporary thinkers seem quite competent and content in their
analyses of either the single individual or the completely universal. From metaphysical thinkers such as Descartes and
Hume, who insist that only individuals *exist,* to social thinkers
such as Hobbes, Rousseau, and Locke, who insist that political and moral rules are based solely on the *rights* of the individual, the conventional wisdom declared the fundamental
metaphysical and political reality of the 'I'. However, later
thinkers such as Kant insisted that morality relied solely on
what is universal, and Hegel went so far as to ground the
entire metaphysical systems of truth in the concrete universal. Thus both Kant and Hegel show us that what is fundamental is the 'All'. The inheritance of both the
Enlightenment's focus on the individual and the idealists' focus on the universal is manifested in our metaphysical and
moral language. We believe in individual rights, but we insist
they are universal; we believe only individuals exist, yet they
constitute various universal systems, from the global ecosys-
tem to the United Nations and the World Bank. We find ourselves speaking either of the sacredness of the one or the
holiness of the all; and sometimes we even seem to think
there is no difference: the one is the all and the all is the one.
The tiniest subatomic particle is isomorphic to the solar system; indeed it *is* a solar system, just as the galaxy is really an
atom.

As awesome as these speculations are, they permit no possible room for the 'we'. It is either 'All' or 'I', and if there is
to be a 'we', it is seen merely as an amalgam of many 'I's' and
is usually deprecated by the censure of unseemly labels:

chauvinism, nationalism, ideologies, totalitarianism, sectarianism, bigotry, racism, sexism, and other fearsome and despised tags that are always seen as impediments to the greatness of individualism on the one hand and the wisdom of world unity on the other. In any event, the 'we' is entirely discredited if not eclipsed by these giant persuasions.

Yet it was not always so. The classical figures recognized not only the autonomy but also the independent worth of the 'we' and affirmed it as a meaningful notion both metaphysically as well as politically. In Plato's *Republic*, for example, Socrates describes the emergence of the ideal state in terms of the three classes, in which the first or citizen class triumphs the benefits to the individual, the 'I'; the second or warrior class triumphs the worth of the community, the 'we'; and the third or ruling class reverses the universal truth of 'all'. But the most important of these three classes is the second class, the warriors, who shift their allegiance from personal benefit to the good in itself. These three classes of the state correspond to the three elements of the soul: appetite, spirit, and mind. Today, if we think of the soul at all, it is seen dualistically: inclination and reason, body and mind, sense and thought, the transient and the eternal. We have universal mind and we have private interests, but, unlike Plato's perfect state or perfect soul, we have no spirit.

But history is a *spiritual* reality: it is neither the result of private interests nor the universal validity of the all of humanity; history is real only if spirit is real; it matters only if there *is* a 'we'.

For the Enlightenment, this 'we' comes about only because of the metaphysical and moral priority of individuals, the sovereign and the citizen, who establish a *contract*. Thus the contract is the foundation of a people and must be seen formally. New contracts can be made, old ones broken, but their meaning relies solely upon the commitment to them of individuals, who then, *after* the signing of the contract, have rights and duties. But for the classical writers, the 'we' is not the *result* of the contract; rather it is the other way around. A people must preexist the making of contracts; indeed a people must preexist the very idea of an individual or a citizen.

The classical idea has never been entirely eclipsed, even during the triumph of the Enlightenment and subsequent Idealism. Thinkers have long persisted in the notion that there is a special status to the 'we' that transcends contracts or individuals. The sketch of these differing philosophical views is made not for the sake of becoming involved in the dispute but merely to show what is at stake in the claims that destiny is essential for history and that *a people* must be assumed if a destiny is possible. What constitutes 'a people' need not be restricted to political or demographic origins. A people may be unified by a religion or ideology, by blood, by race, or by the misadventures of shared defeat; but whatever characterizes their unity, in whatever way, they are always and only a people when they share a common *story*.

And it is the business of historians to tell their story and thereby reveal the uncontrolled destiny that gives meaning to it. We cannot control destiny any more than the gambler controls chance, but without it there is no story at all; and with no story there is no meaning to us as a people.

What ideas have been isolated in this discussion of the historian?

1. History is not a mere chronicle.
2. Neither determinism, nor randomness, nor even blame can account for history.
3. History is a story that has characters, theme, and plot, and that is both *true* and *ours*.
4. The plot of history is destiny, which applies only to peoples.
5. To account for the destiny of peoples, the autonomy of the 'we' must be established.

6. Just as an architect, through his art, changes us from shelter-seekers to dwellers, so the historian, by his telling, changes us from mere elements in a chronology to destined peoples with a meaning.

7. The telling of a story is a meaningful resource of intelligibility, no less so than causes, except that causes explain events and stories explain the meaningfulness of being a people.

4

. . .

THE BIRTHDAY CELEBRANT

Fate as Fortune

"Unto us a son is given."
Handel's *Messiah*

Long before the members of the species were clever enough to figure out the causes and accounts of most physical events, we all seemed to know about the facts of birth. The explanations of a human child being brought into the world are as fundamental and recognizable as any account ever given to any event. Indeed, so primary is this realization that our earliest ancestors explained everything by an appeal to its birth. They asked who the mother of the moon was, who the father of the stars. All the powers and all the things had parents, for the bringing forth of children was what they understood fundamentally, though not scientifically, and hence all else was explained by reference to this first understanding. And yet it never ceases to amaze us. What amazes us, however, is not the 'how' or even the 'why'; rather, it is the 'who'. That is, we find it remarkable that we should exist at all. Indeed, so dazzling is this question of who we are that many fine thinkers dismiss it as a pseudo-question, a problem that vanishes when considered carefully and soberly.

Even so, we celebrate birthdays. We are moved to express this often as a remarkable bestowal, a gift, or at least a wondrous source of awe and reverence. For why should I, or my child, or my beloved, be born at all? This question is simply not answered by the biological and genetic laws that explain it as just another event. Thus the serious inquirer is led to consider the question itself and to wonder just what is being asked. We reflect upon the question, because what is being asked *about* is so wonderfully troubling that we sense distraction in answers that in no way confront our wonder. We want to know how to *think* about what it means for there to be such a notion as 'being born'. And if, in the absence of ready success in such thinking, we are frustrated by our confusion, we make up for this by replacing the satisfaction we would have in understanding with the sheer exuberance of celebration. Because we cannot readily answer the depth of the question, we celebrate the reality.

The celebration of this reality is often carried out by the bestowal of gifts, which is entirely fitting and philosophically significant. We give wages to those who have earned them by contracted labor and rewards to those who have performed deserving deeds, but gifts are given solely on the basis of who one is, as manifestations or celebrations of what it means for the recipient to be at all. The simple phenomenon of gift giving is thus unusually well-designed to elicit from us a sense of what is existentially significant: that *who* we are matters, and not merely what we do. Morally what we earn is more important than what is bestowed, but existentially the hierarchy is reversed.

Yet gift giving on birthdays has an even deeper relevance. For although we know the biological causes of birth, what we celebrate is not this occurrence of natural laws but the mysterious uniqueness of every infant. It is not the 'what' but the 'who' that evokes our gratitude and instinct to bear gifts; and this is due to the profound realization that, although the 'what' is perhaps earned, the 'who' is bestowed. The parents have earned this item of biological process, but they are given the child; and this realization is due in part to the sheer limits of natural explanation. And so we celebrate birthdays.

To understand this more thoroughly we must analyze the two key terms, 'birthdays' and 'celebrate'. It seems curiously satisfying to begin with birth.

THE BIRTHDAY

The question deepens enormously on reflection. To celebrate our birth is to confront the question "why me?" directly. Why should I have been born at all? Why should there *be* a me? The biological account may explain the event, but it cannot throw any light on what it means. "Why me?" Often the interrogative 'why' asks for what purpose or end. "Why did you open the window?" "In order to let in some air." What then is our role? We exist in order to . . . do what? But if we raise the question in this way and insist on asking, "for what purpose was I born?" the inquiry is led entirely astray. The question of a person's purpose presupposes some cosmic scheme that would explain us solely by the roles we play, or were meant to play, in some grand design. This demotes our existence to extrinsic value or a means: I become intelligible solely in terms of my service to the grand plan. If I have a purpose, then my sheer existence is worth nothing and I should be honored only after I have provided this service and certainly not for my mere existence.

If I have a purpose, there should be no celebration of my mere birthday. Obviously, we do play some purposive roles, but they cannot explain the phenomena of birth. It is not my purpose but my private, personal destiny—my 'fortune', if you will—that is celebrated. And this needs to be understood.

The claim is made that my own existence matters uniquely; that is, its worth cannot be supplanted by another and its meaning cannot be replaced or substituted by anyone else.

But why should this claim be made? Surely it would seem more defensible to say that my *achievements* matter, that what I do is for ill or good, but that my sheer existence is simply without worth. And yet even to suggest this is to imply that there is nothing precious about being but only in doing, and that eclipses the entire autonomy of my independent worth. So the question "why me?" does *not* mean "what is my purpose?" but rather "what is my meaning?" And the response is not in the role I play but in the unfolding of my own story, of which the beginning is my birth.

Just as people have a historical destiny, so individuals have a personal destiny, which for the sake of verbal distinction we can provisionally call 'fortune'. But this fortune or personal destiny is not entirely cut off from the intercourse of others. Who I am is answered in part by 'this man's son' or 'that woman's child'; and being a part of a people, our historical destiny is closely interwoven with my personal fortune. Nevertheless, in the celebration of birthdays the emphasis is put on *my* life, which is fundamentally a story, the beginning of which is my birthday. To celebrate the birthday is thus to celebrate my life; but since my life is my story, the celebration is of my story. But a birthday not only initiates the story, it also establishes the 'who'. One cannot inquire into the question "why me?" unless one first knows how to isolate just *'who'* the 'me' is that matters. And so we must ask, how are we to think about the meaning of *who* we are?

And of course the birthday itself gives us a huge "hint" or resource of disclosure. As we have seen, the day celebrates the *birth* of the child, who is, originally, this man's child, that woman's son or daughter. In other words, the simple, unspectacular tradition of birth announcements reveals a great and philosophically wealthy notion: I *am* my inheritance.

At first this means the physical attributes of inheritance that can be noted by the doting parents: "Oh, she has her father's eyes!" That I in no way deserve or am responsible for my skin color, gender, and facial and racial characteristics is of course an important part of my personal fortune. Who I am is influenced as much by these ungoverned and uncontrolled elements of genetic inevitability as the actions I responsibly do. The cultural inheritance is perhaps second only to the physical: that I speak English and that I am protected by decent laws and schooled in wondrous traditions are all a part of my inherited fortune and hence an essential part of my story. Yet over these things I have as little control as the gambler over the roll of dice. Indeed, rather like dice, it is how we are thrown into the world. Are we not then determined by this inheritance? Certainly we are, though this in no way denies responsibility or freedom, because we are free *as* inheritors. This inherited fortune, therefore, provides us with a necessary way of thinking about who we are. Our existence is unintelligible without it.

A birthday is the opening chapter of one's life story. One is not merely a character in the story but also the story itself; for we cannot think of ourselves as characters without a story; indeed, to be a character is already to be in a story. But if we are stories, that is, if we are rendered intelligible in part by the unfolding of narrative meaning, then we are finite, and our having a beginning, middle, and end is necessary for our understanding. Our birth implies our death, and therefore 'who we are' becomes important just because our existence is fleeting.

But nothing is meaningful as change without some unchanging referent. If our brief incursion into the passage of time is to make sense, we must see it in light of whence we come and whither we go: we inherit from our predecessors and bestow what is culturally and spiritually ours to our offspring. To be (as a person) is to inherit; or, to be more precise, to be in time is to be determined by time. This 'determination' is our inheritance, both physical and cultural, which cannot be denied or overcome. Granted some are moved to reject the beginnings, but these rejections merely exacerbate the indebtedness. Some deceive themselves by pretending they are entirely free of any inheritance, forgetting that 'to reject' and 'to pretend' are modes of existence, which themselves are inherited. As long as I articulate my rejection of my inheritance I am using the language I inherit; and even if I learn a new language I use the inherited tongue to learn the new one.

But these may seem little more than observations about the inevitable in the human condition. What is their significance? Precisely because these aspects of our existence cannot be chosen or controlled, it often results in their being dismissed as unworthy of thought. Whatever comes about by the sheer vagaries of nature cannot be seriously considered, only accepted or endured. We seem to be served far better if we simply do not think about them at all. Yet it is their very ungoverned status that makes them so worthy of inquiry. They are interesting in terms not of what brings them about but simply of what they mean. And what *do* they mean? They mean *that, as one who is born, I inherit*. Because of this fortune my existence is intelligible only as a tension between the controlled and the wanton. They also mean that 'to be completely free' is not to be free at all, and that 'to be partly free' is to change entirely what freedom means. Furthermore, 'to be completely determined' is not to be determined at all. The terms entail each other.

To be both free and determined does not mean, as some (such as Kant) would suggest, that in one realm (phenomena) I am entirely determined while in another realm (noumena) I am entirely free. Such divisions merely postpone the confrontation with our truth. It is rather the case that neither term, free or determined, has any meaning whatsoever when postulated absolutely; I also am freely determined and determined to be free, not in one realm or another but in all possible realms. For being *born* I am already on my way to death, and hence the only thing that *can* matter is the passage from the one to the other, my story; and this passage or story unfolds only because my fortune or inheritance provides the ground in which being free is rooted. I am, after all, free only because of who I am—there are none who are free who have no inheritance whatsoever—and hence to see freedom as somehow *opposed* to the determined is mindless. There can be no responsible self (i.e., free self) without an inheritance or fortune; for when I say, "I am responsible for X," the 'I' can only mean this fortuned being who inherits those qualities that make me who I am, one quality being that I and others hold me responsible for what I do. Indeed, when anything happens for which I am not held responsible, to that extent 'I' am not the agent. For the accidental tripping over an electrical wire is not carried out in consequence of my inherited personality or because of my fortune or personal destiny— rather, it is not carried out by *me* at all. To be sure, my foot pulled the wire; but my 'being this man's son or that woman's child' in no way plays a role in explaining the accident. (If I have inherited a certain degree of clumsiness, however, it is then, oddly, that I *might* be held partially responsible; for, aware of my tendency, I should not place myself in such precarious positions.)

Yet, trippings do occur, and if their results are dreadful, an onus falls on me regardless of my innocence, because I am the same man who, being fated, also chooses. To be burdened with uncontrolled and unforeseen events requires an inherited self; to be worthy of praise or blame also requires an inherited self; we can distinguish these events quite easily and need not make any metaphysical presuppositions to do so. They are simply different kinds of events that go to make up my life and my story. The idea, however, that I am responsible only for things I choose to do is absurd, for we are fated to endure our misfortune as surely as to endure censure or to bask in praise. If I am honored for my intelligence but dishonored because I use it for nefarious purposes, it is the same 'me' who is both honored and dishonored. Granted that *morally* I do not deserve praise for my gifts but do deserve whatever praise or blame I get because of my usage of them, the *existential* meaning of my natural gifts is intimately tied up with how and for what purpose I use them. The key point here is that it is the same 'I' in all cases, and thus 'I' came into existence burdened and favored with fortune, at my *birth*. Hence even my freely deserved acts of goodness are grounded in this unfolding character-in-a-plot, and thus to celebrate my birth is to affirm this primordial realization.

It is this metaphysical proliferation of 'I's' that is unacceptable. If there is only one 'I' that both acts freely *and* endures the wantonness of fortune and misfortune, then 'being free' and 'being determined' are not inconsistent but complementary modes or ways of passing through the allotted duration of my story. 'Who I am' is thus perhaps replaceable by 'what is the unfolding of my story', which is made intelligible by the equally fundamental notions of being responsible and having an inheritance or fortune.

My parents celebrated my birth when I was a child because I was theirs, and *being* theirs I have inherited their physical and cultural traits. The highly developed sense of responsibility I have is also due, in part, to this inheritance; but because I have also inherited critical skills I can also project beyond these limits to some extent; and as I grow older and become more responsible for how I deal with these inheritances the celebration of my birth encloses this maturation as a part of who I am and what is celebrated.

In my being born *as* a male, American, white, and so on, I am fated to be male and American and white not because I opted for these by choice but simply because I inherited them. The logical absurdity of somehow first existing and then choosing what *kind* of thing or person I am to become reveals that who I am is necessarily characterized by fate. To celebrate my birth is therefore to celebrate my fate or fortune, but also to celebrate my independence of them.

If one imagines an unbroken chain of generations in which certain traits or characteristics are passed on from parent to offspring, such an image reveals much of what we mean by inheritance and fortune but nothing at all of individuality and uniqueness. Yet each person in the chain, inheriting and passing on traits, has special significance, not merely because of morally responsible acts but also because their place in the chain accounts, in part, for who they are. Birth begins not only a new link in the chain but also a possibility of responsibility and guilt. Thus I do not "possess" my fortune; I *am* my fortune, since my fortune is not only what I inherit but also what I do with it. This is what is celebrated in birthdays.

CELEBRATION

From outside the stadium a mighty roar of awesome amplitude could be heard. Moments later the fans poured out into the streets, yelling, screaming, gesticulating, and jumping up and down. The home team had won the championship game. Almost every fan was drinking beer from cans, and some with a remarkable capacity for absorption. They did not know what to yell, so most of the sounds were simply variations of the first vowel, in wordless abandon of any attempt to articulate. Occasionally a chant would start somewhere in the crowd, which in feral rhythm would suddenly find acceptance by the throng, and one could note their willingness to unify briefly by this invocation of the same mindless sounds. They were obviously elated. There was also an undeniable sense of sharing in the sweetness of victory and an unusual bonding among themselves and the achievements of the beloved, though absent, athletes. They kept shouting, "We won," as if this vast congregation of throaty thousands had actually defeated the opposition. None could deny their happiness. None could honestly begrudge them their festive mood. But no one could truthfully say that these people knew how to celebrate.

Celebration can be a success or a failure. We are celebrating beings, but this does not mean all celebrations are equally well done. Indeed, one can even fail at celebrating altogether. Because of this we can legitimately imply that there are standards of celebration that can be met or broken; but if there are standards, as well as degrees of success, it also means that the phenomenon is capable of analysis and judgment; that is, it can be thought about.

Celebration can also be denied altogether. The New England colonists made a point of refusing to celebrate the Christian holidays, for these festivities reminded our stern forefathers of popish decadence. Thus celebration is made intelligible by its contrasts: sobriety, decency, decorum, *gravitas*, and grim propriety. The Nietzschean distinction between Dionysian and Apollonian spirits is a helpful resource, as is my earlier contrast between Brutus and Antony. In short, celebration is a notion of profound philosophical significance, and, though this present analysis is far too brief to do it justice, it is worthy of study for its own sake and not merely, as now, to help us understand the birthday celebrant.

One point should be made clear at the onset. The etymology of the term, from the Latin *celeber*, meaning 'frequented' or 'populous', suggests the communal nature of celebration: it is a gathering together of the people to honor or to esteem someone or an event of importance for the group. Strictly, then, one cannot celebrate alone. And this is why the celebration of birthdays is so fitting, for the feted one is accepted into the fold, as it were; the rejoicing is because the child is *ours*, as the famous line from Handel's *Messiah* sings: "Unto *us* a son is *given*."

This unity with a people is noted in the tradition of celebrating by imbibing the merrier spirits: in the intoxication of the Dionysian, the sense of communal unity is contrasted

with the sober individual. With the fruit of the vine we become as one people because our calculative skills, which produce private or personal interests, are dulled, and a warm
sense of camaraderie prevails.

But if intoxication is essential for the Dionysian, who embodies celebration, then why is the drunken display of high
spirits outside the stadium designated a failure in celebration?
The etymology and traditional understanding of the term emphasize not the drunkenness but the *ritualism* of celebration.
To celebrate in this sense is to perform a rite, made sacred by
its antiquity and custom. Which institutions are recognized as
knowing how to celebrate? Who can deny that the British
government, especially in tribute of its sovereigns, produces
the grandest shows? The Roman Catholic and Eastern Ortho-
dox churches do so also. But these are successful just because
they are rituals, long determined by traditions and solem-
nized by time. A true celebration is a rite, in which the actions, gestures, and festivities are all meaningful, especially
in the communal sense, and are even *performative,* in the
sense that they do not merely recall an event to mind but,
like a promise or a marriage, actually create the order that is
revered and esteemed.

To emphasize this role of communal acceptance as a part of
celebration, many religious groups prefer to celebrate not
birthdays but the days on which people are baptized and
given names. To be named is to enter as a meaningful member into the community, and such an event is celebrated
simply because, as a performative ritual, it gathers together a
people in praise of their destiny, integrating the communal
story with the personal fortune of the one named or born.

These reflections now congeal into a wondrous paradox. To
celebrate is to call a people together to perform a ritual in
which the festive elicits a triumph of their destiny. But a
birthday singles out an individual, trumpets the worth of the
one among the whole, so that the one is not eclipsed by the
membership in the community, nor is the communal sacri-

ficed by the elevation of the one. Being one matters only as being among the others, and being among the others matters only as being one. The historical destiny of the entire people gathers its resources of rites and rituals to celebrate the inherited fortune of the single member whose birth matters uniquely as the beginning of a personal, private destiny. Without the ritual traditions of a people's destiny, there could be no celebration at all, yet what is celebrated is the singularity of one, free member. What we are calling 'fortune', that is, personal destiny, is honored and ultimately made possible by the people's tradition granted as an inheritance. We rejoice in being who we are, and this rejoicing makes us unique.

This is of great philosophical importance because we need to know how to think about who we are. This thinking has two opposing origins: that I matter because of my responsibility and that I matter because of my inheritance—this woman's child, that man's son, this culture's preserver, and that society's citizen. In each of these four ways I am responsible not only for what I do but also for what I am, even though over these inheritances I have had neither control nor option. The philosopher must struggle to work out how thinking this is possible; but those who celebrate birthdays perform the reality of it in simple but profound rites. Those incapable of rejoicing in their inheritance are just as unfree as those whose chains restrain their choices and limit their responsibility.

Earlier in this inquiry it was suggested that fate may possibly have a purely moral meaning, contrasting who I am as responsible with who I am as fated. But these present considerations show this contrast to be too simplistic. The simple fact that I have inherited the color of my skin and eyes, and hence could not choose them, has been revealed as a much deeper modality of my existence, that only as fated can I matter at all and only if I matter can I be free. For being free fundamentally depends on my being responsible; but I cannot *be* responsible unless *who* I am first matters.

The question raised earlier, "why should there be a *me* at

all?" is here given philosophical foundation. The 'why' is revealed as a question of meaning, and the 'me' is shown to consist of fated responsibility. Insofar as my peculiar destiny or fortune is ungoverned, I cannot seek for determinant *causes,* for the appeal to the biological and genetic laws explains everyone, and hence what is unique is lost; or, rather, it is either lost or trivialized. Indeed, were I able to give either purposive or causal accounts, such fated elements would cease to be interesting or meaningful. At the same time, although I cannot *determine* such inheritance, I am a responsible being because of who I am, and that just means *being* fated.

This realization in no way changes the moral law, nor does it in any way extenuate my guilt or render ethical prohibitions relative. On the contrary, we discover in these reflections a more profound sense of responsibility, one grounded not in the happy circumstances of various alternatives that I select, like choosing items from a menu, but in the deepest realization of who I am and whence I came. Only as named can I be truly free, and the celebration of the day of naming is the affirmation of my inheritance—so it is precisely because I do *not* name myself that I am myself. Because I am fated to be me I can be who I am, and *as* who I am only can I be free.

These reflections, though insightful, may appear somewhat random. Suppose the question of who I am is raised in a more methodical manner. To ask who I am may possibly be illuminated by considering the range of possible elements that make me who I am. There seem to be five different resources or elements that go to make up what might be called my 'character'. They are as follows:

1. What I inherit simply as a member of the species. Thus, for example, I am a rational being, a being with a memory, a central nervous system, and so on. These are common to all humans.

2. What I inherit as 'this man's son, that woman's child'. These are things such as my racial, sexual, and genetic characteristics that I receive from the purely biological origins of my parents. Although these are not shared by all people as are the first kind of characteristics, they are nonetheless explainable by natural laws.

3. What I inherit as a member of this culture and tradition. My language, early beliefs and values, and loyalties to my spiritual legacy belong to me as surely as does the color of my skin.

4. What I have learned from experience up till now, as well as what effect my responses to these experiences have imported to me. We might label this class of characteristics my education and environment. Surely who I am is determined in part by these influences.

5. What I contribute to my character by my responsible acts, including the guilt, shame, pride, and honor that affect me as a result. Apparently these are so-called 'free' acts.

These resources seem to be, if not exclusive, at least the major classes of qualities that characterize or determine who I am. The fifth, however, is possible only because of the first four and indeed cannot ever be isolated from the impact and persuasion of the earlier qualities on the list. Thus, for example, a brutal and severe childhood may well influence the extent to which one would be persuaded by the dictates of reason, so that such a one might be less 'free' than one favored by more congenial surroundings.

The question that now arises is this: does this list of five kinds of influence *exhaust* the possible ways of thinking about who I am? In other words, if I know all five, do I then know *me*? Or is it the case that this list, or any list, always presupposes the very thing being considered, namely me? Are these five kinds of influence mere predicates of the original 'I', or are they the actual and exhaustive *elements* that can be said quite literally to make up or to constitute who I am? If they are but predicates, then the question is, how are we to think of the subject (I) that contains these attributes? However, if they constitute elements that adequately account for the 'I', then there is nothing left to wonder about once these are fully considered.

To celebrate a birth is to deny the latter and affirm the former. In an older tradition with a richer if perhaps more mythical language, there was a 'soul' that was *given* to us by a bestowing God; "unto us a child is given." If we bracket these metaphysical and theological terms, however, we still retain this sense of bestowed fortune that is the legacy of birthdays: we are given.

If we accept the five-part list above and recognize that the fifth class (free acts) presupposes the first four (inheritance and experience), we now add a sixth, which presupposes the first five and culminates the entire hierarchy: we are bestowed.

There is, however, an even deeper significance to this listing. It might be thought that the physical and cultural influences of my inheritance are capable of being reasoned or thought about solely by reference to causal accounts, that is, by an appeal to the natural laws. Only the fifth and sixth items would be rendered intelligible by an appeal to moral principles or to existential principles that render the meaning of existence intelligible. This would be erroneous, however, for the *entire* list, from one through five (or even six), is about the meaning of existence. We are asking what it *means* to be fated, and the uncontrolled or thrown dimensions of items one through four on the list are to be understood as fundamental ways in which my unchosen fortune contributes to the comprehension of what it means to exist as fated. Thus my fortune or private destiny is not to be seen as made up of factors that are accountable by scientific methodologies, for *as* fortune they illuminate what it means for me to be *me*. To be sure, the biological factors that determine my genetic characteristics are, as biology, intelligible as science, just as the environmental factors are intelligible as sociology and hence in terms of human science (if there is such a thing). But what it means to be so determined is not a scientific question but a philosophical one. The established disciplines of science and morality may explain *that* I am genetically determined or morally restricted, but what it means to be moral and to be natural remains an existential question. Thus, to claim that I am bestowed, or that I am thrown into the world beyond my option as white, male, and left-handed, remains fundamentally a philosophical, existential reality, open only to the kind of inquiry that seeks ontological meaning in the analysis of modalities of what it means to exist.

As the gambler reveals the significance of luck and fate and the historian manifests the bestowal of destiny, so the birthday celebrant concretizes the existential inevitability of fated freedom in terms of fortune or inheritance. The study of the birthday and why we celebrate it becomes a fundamental resource for inquiring into the awesome question "why me?"

What has this analysis of the birthday celebrant revealed?

1. The celebration of birthdays by the honored tradition of giving gifts mirrors the fundamental ontological truth that our fortune (i.e., our private, fated inheritance) is a bestowal.
2. Our fortune is not opposed to our freedom but is a necessary presupposition for it.
3. This inheritance is an essential and nonreducible part of our understanding of who we are; that is, I cannot disjoin the meaning of my existence *from* my fortune.
4. Celebration is a fundamental part of who we are.
5. Celebration is a source both of communality as well as uniqueness.

6. The elements that make up our unchosen fortune are not understandable solely in terms of causal determinism; that is, to be 'this man's son and that woman's child' has existential and not merely biological significance.

These six discoveries are of critical importance in the analysis of our fate. But one final character or model needs to be explored before we can synthesize these insights into a truly philosophical response to the question "why me?" We must turn now to the drama, the most vivid of all the images of fate.

CHAPTER

5
∎ ∎ ∎

THE TRAGEDIAN
Fate as Inevitability

Few human experiences, aesthetic or otherwise, equal the impact of a good performance of a great tragedy. Other arts may be more beautiful, other genres may be more pleasing, and much of what is endured in daily conflict is more useful. But tragedies have an uncanny power to unsettle and to disturb. When the curtain falls on Shakespeare's *King Lear* or Sophocles' *Oedipus Tyrannos*, there is an inescapable realization that a dreadful truth, as if hitherto secret and reserved only for the elect, has been exposed to us, the audience, forever altering who we are and who we will be. We, the audience, become tragic sufferers along with the hero on the stage. It is as if a sacred mystery has been violated, so that what should have remained a privilege of knowledge only for the anointed few has been made available to a public that is too weak to endure the burden of this weighty truth. Fate is the discloser of this sanctum, and, having it so nakedly revealed, we are stunned with an awe that is almost religious. Perhaps indeed it is religious.

To be sure, tragedy is an art form with its roots in religious ritual; it is not an actual phenomenon: neither the actors nor the audience actually endure the dreadful torments depicted on the stage. There is much to be gained in realizing that this 'aesthetic distance', rather than relieving us of the immediacy of suffering, actually serves as an intensifier of its meaning. Like the window pane that protects us from the ravages of the pelting storm and thereby allows us to experience awe and sublimity that sheer prudential concerns deny to the actual victim in the storm, so the separation of the audience from the anguish actually allows a closer, more intimate confrontation of what it means to be tragically fated. This distance, however, does not, as some seem to argue, provide us with the relief that it is others, and not us, who must endure, for the ritual performance links us more intimately with the heroic suffering than it contrasts. Indeed, in good performances we seem to be able to endure the anguish but not experience it. The aesthetic diversity of theories on tragedy, fascinating as they are, need not intrude into this analysis, however. For the sole purpose of focusing on the tragedian's art is to understand how we *think* about what it means to be tragically fated and from this analysis to come to grips with fate.

Tragedy begins in the religious celebration of the ancient Athenian festival of Dionysos, and much of the religious impact of the ritual remains even in the modern representations of the ceremonial rite. It is only of the tragedies actually performed on a real stage that I speak of here, not the tragic stories read in textbooks or even the slick filmed versions of what are quaintly known as the classics. The impact is reserved for audiences, not for readers; and, for the few who are receptive to this singular art form, nothing is quite as overwhelming or as troubling.

It is not merely disturbing because we seem to applaud the suffering of great men and women, though that remains a source of puzzlement; rather, it is the unexpected enormity of the truth revealed that makes us wonder and return. We realize something of spectacular importance has taken place, that our deepest levels, whatever they are, have been irresistibly stirred and our wonder excited. Yet we also sense that we have been bestowed more with a question than with an answer, that our minds are now in turmoil with a dissatisfaction at our ignorance. It is thus a stimulus to philosophic thought.

Indeed, philosophy, along with comedy, is a gift, accompanying tragedy, from the Dionysians. So it is not unexpected that of all the art forms, tragedy alone has provoked the most persistent interest and analysis by their fellow Dionysians, the philosophers, throughout the centuries, ever since Aeschylus first introduced the second player. In part, of course, this is due simply to the irresistible fact that there is, in the attendance of a tragic sacrament, a massive paradox, questioning why men of decency and standing seem to take such huge delight in the witnessing of dreadful suffering. But it is also due to the power of tragedy to reveal truth, far more than any other art form, that so provokes the thinker.

And so we not only attend the plays of Sophocles and Shakespeare but also read the treatises of Aristotle and Nietzsche. It is not enough to have the impact of Antigone or Othello; we also want the justification from the wisest among us, to tell us what it means. Tragedy and philosophy have always been mutual sources of illumination, and to understand either of these disciplines fully this interdependence must be understood.

And yet the justifications of the wise do not seem to honor the achievements of the muse. In seeking to understand our bewilderment in witnessing the downfall of Oedipus, we find that Aristotle justifies the hero's suffering by an appeal to a tragic flaw, that the hubris of the great has transgressed his limits, offending the *sophrosone* of the people. We are told that the hero's anguish is justified because the catharsis of the artwork has cleansed us from the sentiments of fear and pity. Oedipus was, after all, a parricide and guilty of incest; his doom is but the inevitable triumph of justice.

There can be no doubt that the witnessing of triumphant justice elates us highly. When the curtain falls on a performance of Beethoven's *Fidelio,* for example, the passions and emotions are clear and wonderful. One not only delights in seeing good triumph and evil fail, one also feels morally uplifted by these achievements of justice. It is a good and wondrous thing to feel these lofty sentiments of joy. So overwhelming is this conviction that Nahum Tate, in the untragic eighteenth century, rewrote the final act of *King Lear* so that Cordelia and her father ultimately triumph over the villains in the play. This rewriting justifies the theory, perhaps. But we know we are beguiled by these triumphs. For although the moralist justification undoubtedly makes sense in explaining why we should rejoice, the account in no way seems adequate to the impact of the artistic truth. We simply do not leave the tragic theater feeling that justice is vindicated. Perhaps the discovery of achieved justice does indeed elate, but such elation does not seem to be the result of watching the great tragic plays.

There are, of course, other justifications. For Hegel the justification of enormous human suffering lies in the dialectical emergence of the historical synthesis: we delight even as we grieve because the unfolding truth triumphs a greater intellectual vision of who we are. At least Hegel recognizes that it is not merely justice that is trumpeted; in spotting truth as the victor we are at least relieved of having to indict or to censure the undiscoverable 'tragic flaw' of a noble Antigone. Yet even his justification seems inadequate to account for the impact.

Nietzsche may bring us even closer by his account of the conflicting marriage between the Apollonian and Dionysian spirits. But does this magnificent justification in any way render the torment that we share endurable? Schopenhauer tells us that tragedy shows us the triumph of the human spirit over the inevitability of the World Will. Does even this justify our

THE TRAGEDIAN   ·   93

passionate grief at the collapse of Othello's marriage with the innocent Desdemona? Granted, these wise and insightful men have contributed much to our understanding of tragedy, but have they, as they claim, justified our applause of human failure? The impact still remains greater than these justifications.

Perhaps this is because tragedy, like fate, cannot be justified. Whatever can be justified, whether morally, metaphysically, or theologically, just is not tragedy anymore. In the same way that a theodicist in justifying evil by appealing to God's greater wisdom in fact denies that any real evil actually exists, so any account of tragedy that seeks to explain our appreciation of the artwork by somehow justifying the suffering actually renders the suffering *deserved,* and hence a boon, which is precisely what we cannot and do not accept in the face of the tragic resolution. But if we cannot justify the tormented misery of the tragic hero, then how can we accept our own applause? How can we render our appreciation of the play acceptable?

Indeed it is precisely because the anguish is *unjustified* that the tragic impact is so remarkable. All attempts to justify the hero's suffering succeed only in defanging the monster. We come to see not justified suffering but unjustified suffering; and if the intellectuals convince us otherwise, the tragic genius is wasted. But with this realization the paradox threatens to overcome us with sheer incomprehensibility. Is this madness?

We do not come to the theater to see great men fail; rather, we come to see greatness revealed or even achieved through failure. We come not to see the noble suffer but to watch suffering ennoble. Thus it is not the suffering that needs to be justified but the nobility that needs to be confronted, and only the magnitude of the suffering can accomplish this. But if we can be ennobled by torment, then we are confronted with a great and awesome truth, a truth that elevates far more successfully than the elation we may experience at witnessing justice triumph. For in tragedy it is justice that is sacrificed—and we sacrifice only that which is dear—to esteem a great honor. The dignity of one rendered noble by unendurable hardship, showing us most nakedly the exposed truth that who we are, even if unadorned by *any* success whatsoever, can indeed *matter.* This is the true and only glory of the tragic art.

In order to measure this, however, we must note carefully just what the tragedian *does.* He deliberately sabotages all of our normal instincts for vindication and justice, all of our decent impulses to reward with favors those who excel, and even defeats our predisposition to fit the plot to the character. Rather, the tragedian unravels his plot to thwart our goodly expectations, turning fate and circumstance, villainy and foolishness, against the one who matters most. But he must do this with a deftness and artistry almost unsurpassed among other artisans, for he must accomplish all of these inversions of reward without rendering his hero into a victim; he must torment and punish and unfairly deny all solace and surcease, yet leave the hero or heroine unpitied. There are few successful tragedians because there cannot be mediocre or even fairly good tragedians. The great is their milieu, and hence they are few.

What is accomplished by this artistic genius? Even if successful, why does the tragedian isolate the hero from all success? Precisely to show that the noble do not need success to emerge worthy of our awe. But this is to say that existence in and of itself can matter; it is to show that *who* we are counts as much, if not more, than what we do or what happens to us. What we do and what happens to us together constitute the realm of success; it is the field of justice, it is the range of hope for happiness. But it is not the *only* range of human concern. Or rather, it can, by a greatness found in the Dionysian hierarchy, be surpassed. If *we* matter, as well as what we do matters, then success cannot be the sole determiner of human worth.

Because of this rupture from success, the tragedian must depend less on his plot and more on his character. Plots dominate moral stories, characters existential ones. To be sure, the plot must be carefully chosen, for it must provide two essential elements: it must create first suspense and secondly inevitability. Only wickedly ingenious plotting can do this, for if the suspense is overly stressed, the audience develops an intense desire for successful resolution, and the tragic ending will merely frustrate; however, if the inevitability drowns all suspense, the interest ceases to be dramatic and becomes boringly pedantic. Nevertheless, the plotting is in service of the character development, for the 'who' remains the focus of this Dionysian art. An example may be illuminating.

Antigone and her sister Ismene are caught in as cruel a dilemma as the cunning of Sophocles can contrive. Their uncle Creon, the king, has forbidden their brother, Polyneices, to be buried because he rebelled against the legitimate authority of the state; but their religion demands that their brother be buried in order for his soul to achieve rest and salvation. Regardless of which way they act, the sisters must offend one of two very powerful institutions, the state or religion, the king or the gods. Added to this is their natural love for their own kinsmen, uncle and brother, making it impossible for them to avoid harming someone they love in their own family. Antigone buries her brother, but Ismene obeys her kingly uncle. Are we to understand by this outcome that, since the play bears Antigone's name, we are to prefer brothers to uncles or the law of the gods to the law of the state? To argue this way is to miss the greatness of the play entirely. Antigone stands out not because of her choice but because of her nobility. The play is named after her not because of what she does but because of who she is.

Ismene, after all, is in a similar position. She, too, is

doomed regardless of her choice. Is it possible for a great playwright to create a tragedy called *Ismene* in which a noble niece boldly rejects her religious obligation in order to serve her king and uncle? Of course it is. But the character of Ismene could not be the same as that so brilliantly sketched out by Sophocles. Ismene would have to manifest that same noble spirit, that same bold acceptance of fate, that same splendor of pride in who one is that Antigone displays in Sophocles' tragedy. There simply is no moral message at all in tragedy; it is rather an art form that celebrates the autonomy of the character's worth from the wretchedness of the character's fortune. And an essential element of the tragic character is the passionate reverence for truth, especially as it is unfolded in the inevitability of one's fate. Schopenhauer is thus very close, but profoundly wrong, in his analysis; it is not the peaceful resignation to the World Will that shows the hero's triumph over it, for there is nothing resigned or peaceful about Antigone or Othello or Macbeth; but there is a bold acceptance of the *truth*, so essential for genuine nobility, that is evident in the embrace of a cruel fate that bestows meaning; and in this bestowal fate reveals itself as essential for our understanding of the tragic hero.

Tragedy therefore, by sabotage of success, isolates the noble character and makes us glad not that Lear suffers but simply that there *is* a Lear, made who he is in part by his torment. But Ismene, in Sophocles' play, also suffers, yet she is not tragic. Why? Not because of her choice, as we have seen. It is thus possible to suffer and *not* become noble. It is possible to achieve unsuccess and yet still not be tragic. The art form is not a how-to book, telling us the steps we must take in order to achieve the status of greatness. This would be simply to substitute terms, justifying tragic greatness rather than tragic goodness. But there is no justification in tragedy at all. There is only denuding. There is the mere manifestation that who one is can matter. Not that 'who one is' *always* matters; simply that it *can* matter. Or rather, to be more precise, Oedipus matters, Antigone matters, Lear matters; but Ismene does not, Iago does not, Albany does not.

Tragedy must be seen as an existential art form, not a moral one. As I show in an article published by *Man and World* in 1988, only by refusing to read tragedies as moral lessons can one appreciate the effort taken by the artist to isolate our existential worth. Though this sets the fundamental stage for the interpretation, it is nevertheless only the first step. In a chapter entitled "Fate" in my later work *Truth and Existence,* I discovered a further and perhaps even more decisive insight into our understanding of tragedy. For this great art form is not merely a celebration of autonomous existential worth but also an engine of fated inevitability, in which the unfolding of destined truth reveals the meaning of who we are.

Any sensitive witness to a well-presented tragedy will confess to the achieved sense of irresistible doom that seems to wash the hapless figure in a current of misfortune. Even if we are unfamiliar with the story, we know what dire news the messenger to Oedipus will bring, that Friar Laurence's envoy will not reach Mantua in time, that Desdemona will not retrieve her handkerchief. Essential to the very *craft* of tragedy is the curious blend of suspense and doom with which the narrative unfolds its grim inevitability. The better the playwright, the clearer this sense that the ensuing disaster simply cannot be avoided, that given the character of the protagonist the fall must surely come. This is a palpable fact discernible in the art form; our present task is to understand what it means. Granted that the artistry of the tragedian convinces us of the character-grounded inevitability of tragedy, why should this be the case? How are we to understand it?

We must first distinguish 'predictability' from 'inevitability'. To say that the grim resolution of tragedies is inevitable is not to say that one can predict the behavior of those who possess heroic qualities. Prediction properly belongs to science, and to equate this with tragic inevitability is to transfer the understanding of the art form to the psychologist. There is no doubt one can predict that sugar will dissolve in water; perhaps we may even predict that abused children will statistically be more inclined to be adult abusers; it *may* even be possible to predict specific behavior of a specific individual if the traumatic history has been severe and the causal agencies well known. But in no way does the tragic artist intend for us to believe that the actions of an Oedipus or a Lear can be predicted, scientifically, following the measured authority and grim assurance of the natural law. For this would make the unfolding of the drama as irresistible as the unwinding of a clock, and as uninteresting.

But what, then, does 'inevitability' mean if it is not to be equated with predictability? We have already seen that in tragic plays we confront an unfolding drama in which the grim results seem to be thought of as somehow following from the kind of personality possessed by the protagonist; that is, we observe the events taking place in a way that reflects— perhaps even mirrors—our understanding of who the hero is. But is not this precisely what we do in science? Knowing the characteristics of sugar we see the actual fact of it dissolving in water as a natural consequence of its nature. How is this different? For one thing, the link between the subject and the ensuing event is not causal. We do not say that Oedipus's character *causes* him to gouge out his eyes; we merely say that this gruesome violence is accepted as a dramatic consequence of who Oedipus is. But does the mere sequestering of the term 'cause' suffice to establish such an important difference? When we probe more deeply we discover that 'tragic inevitability' does not entail a sense of logical necessity, for Oedipus remains understood as a morally responsible, that is, free, agent. Yet we do seem to suggest that if Oedipus were to have acted otherwise the drama would be neither as compelling nor as coherent. We may dismiss the 'compulsion' as a purely aesthetic accomplishment, but the 'coherence' speaks of a stronger claim. There is, in other words, a 'rightness' about the cruel infliction on the protagonist; indeed, so persuasive is this sense of rightness that Aristotle was led to account for it by appealing to justice. But we have sequestered justice from our account and are now claiming that it is more than merely aesthetic propriety. Perhaps there is an 'existential' sense of rightness, a kind of fitness to the story that comes from our understanding of what it means to exist. But what else is this except our ordinary understanding of fate?

The analysis, however, has apparently reversed itself entirely. In the earlier chapters fate was described as almost wanton and uncontrolled randomness that resisted all attempts at governance and justification. Now we seem to be suggesting that fate is indeed governed, and by no less an authorative concept than that of the character or personality of the hero in the drama. If the fate of Oedipus follows from his character, then it is entirely dissimilar to the random fortuities of the gambler, and equally unlike the sheer inheritance of the birthday celebrant.

Nevertheless, the weight of the inquiry must be duly carried out. There is no doubt that great tragedies do indeed provide the audience with a sense of inevitability that seems rooted in the character of the tragic hero; and there is no doubt that the inevitable linkage between the gruesome unsuccess of the hero and the hero's character seems to unfold as a manifestation of fate. If this seems to make the gambler's fate different from the tragic sufferer's fate, we must perforce accept this and try to come to grips with it rather than to dissemble with tricks or with unseemly avoidance of the difficulty.

Predictability assumes that to know the antecedent condition is to know the consequent and to know the cause is to know the effect. If I know the battery in the flashlight is active, I know the light will glow when I press the switch. But with tragic inevitability, the death of Lear is realized as fitting only after Shakespeare has unfolded the drama. We might therefore think that our sense of inevitability is the result of the artist's skill in telling the story; that by 'inevitability' we mean that Shakespeare has succeeded in his craft, which is to make us *feel* that the deaths of Cordelia and Lear follow inevitably by some peculiar aesthetic logic from the influences of their characters and the cruel twists of fate. And we would be correct in thinking this, for, after all, tragedy is not real life but an art form, and we appreciate it because the artist has designed it to be appreciated. This is correct as far as it goes. What needs to be added, however, is that tragedy is not merely an aesthetic genre that delights us; it is also a source of truth. Tragedy has not only aesthetic but also veridical value. Furthermore, it must be questioned *why* we feel this inevitability and why to feel it gives us such rare satisfaction.

It is not enough simply to point out that the audience is convinced Lear's death is inevitable; we must ask how and why. To be sure, this inevitability is discovered *only* in the art form. But this does not imply, as so many critics think, that therefore this sense of the inevitable is *merely* aesthetic. (What does 'merely' mean here anyway? Does it mean that what is learned through art has no veridical ground? But that is absurd. Art is art *because* it reveals truth, at times in a superior fashion to experience.) We take enormous satisfaction in the unfolding of tragic inevitability precisely because this unfolding is self-revealing; from it we learn about who we are. We see that even to be the plaything of wanton fortune is to outlast our miseries; that because our suffering, represented in the tragedy, follows from our character, we cannot dismiss the suffering without eclipsing our character. Who we are matters, and if this 'who' is shown to be linked *inevitably* to our suffering, even if undeserved, then this suffering no longer threatens the intelligibility of our existence.

For what is the threat? Is it not that our undeserved suffering can so overcome our capacity to make sense of things that in enduring these ills we find our existence bereft of meaning? We have seen that theodicistic justification of evil contradicts the meaning of evil, as do all justifications outside of sacrifice and justice itself. Thus, to suffer unduly is an offense against *reason* and prompts both misology and nihilism. But tragedy depicts undue suffering as a form of narrative coherence; on the stage the 'who' of the fated hero is revealed as radiant and fundamental, exposed by the denuding stripes of indifferent fortune. Thus the hero is curiously revealed as *mattering* even when all elements of success are denied. This does not provide some naive solace for the suffering shared by all in the audience; it is rather a triumph of Dionysian spirit that allows *thought* and not mere *feeling* to occur. On the one hand, tragedy assures us that who we are simply outranks what happens to us. (The presence of King Lear is never eclipsed by his ample misfortune.) On the other hand, the very fact of fate becomes a source of illumination for who we are. Our existence stands out the more our life is darkened. This, however, is never to be seen as a justification, for the moment we think of it *as* justification, the tragic disappears. It is precisely because these woeful miseries cannot be justified that they are seen as truly fated. To ground these fates in character, as Heraclitus suggests, is not to render character the *cause*, nor is it to render the suffering *justified*. It is rather to *isolate* the *worth* of character from our deserved happiness, to say that 'who we are' is not dependent on our success. It would be fundamentally nihilistic to judge the worth of our existence solely or even chiefly by the amount of our happiness at our success. To believe I matter only if I succeed is to deny that I matter at all; it is to say that only the good things that happen to me can matter. Of course, if only the good things that happen to me matter, then should misfortune arise my entire worth is forfeit, and *that* dismal judgment is simply unacceptable. Tragedy shows this not to be true, and so we applaud.

In *Thus Spoke Zarathustra,* Nietzsche protests in the prologue that our greatest moment is when our happiness and virtue are rejected as disgusting and contemptuous. Why should Zarathustra say such a thing? Why does our own happiness fill us with contempt? Because, Nietzsche assures us, our happiness does not justify our existence. For, if happiness is what matters, then our existence is meaningful only when and because we are happy. But this is to deny that existence itself, unadorned by happiness, has any meaning. To realize this is to be filled with contempt. It is not by accident that Nietzsche initiates his philosophical quest into the meaning of existence by a study of tragedy.

Yet even with this discovery the mystery of tragedy has not been fully developed. Earlier I raised the problem of Antigone's poor sister, Ismene. I said that although her dilemma is the same as Antigone's and she too was beguiled by the cruelty of fate, she is not, for all that, a tragic hero. Why? What is it that Antigone possesses that Ismene does not? To witness the play is to recognize this difference, for Sophocles' genius makes Antigone radiant and Ismene dreary with spiritual defeat. Again we seem to be entirely at the mercy of the tragedian's art: the very language of Richard II gives him a tragic status, which the more politically astute Bolingbroke lacks. Is then a tragic hero made so merely because the artist has put more glorious language on his tongue than on others'?

Formally, of course, the distinction between Antigone and Ismene is simply that the latter judges her misfortune to be more important than who she is, whereas Antigone realizes that who she is outranks her terrible suffering. But if this difference is itself grounded simply in *who* Antigone is and *who* Ismene is, we must seek a deeper understanding. The clue the tragedian gives is usually—indeed almost always among the greatest of them—that of language. In a play, the nobles are identified by the nobility of their speech. In *Richard II*, during the quarrel in act I, the future king, Henry Boling-broke, speaks more nobly than the worthy but unkingly Mow-bry. By such a simple iconographic device Shakespeare works a wonder of dramaturgy.

But why language? Is it because language is, after all, the medium of the dramatic artist? Or is it because tragedy just attracts poetic dramatists? Perhaps. But there is a more profound reason: it is through language that truth is revealed, and 'being true to truth' is the ultimate ontological meaning of nobility. And so we can now suggest that just as the halo is the iconographic device medieval painters use to designate sanctity, so nobility of language is that which designates the tragic hero. In both cases there is a deeper meaning: the halo signifies inner radiance, a glowing that provides a beacon for the bewildered sinner. Noble language is found only in noble souls, and the foundational understanding of nobility is esteem for truth, which language alone can provide.

■   ■   ■

These are the factors that we learn from studying the *craft* of the tragedian, that is, how he goes about his work. They can be summarized as follows:

1. The tragedian deliberately sabotages success in order to let the worth of sheer existence be denuded.
2. But not just anyone can be a tragic hero, so the tragedian focuses on the nobility of the character, usually by giving the noble hero the most radiant language.
3. The tragedian develops a sense of inevitability, sometimes even by telling us the entire plot in a prologue, to

focus on the power of fate. This inevitability is not the same as predictability.

4. The tragedian uses the plot to enhance the character, and not vice versa.
5. The tragedian never *justifies* the suffering of the hero, but does illuminate it.
6. The tragedian works not to make the noble suffer but to make suffering noble.

But what do these six points tell us about fate? Have they not completely reversed the discoveries of the last three analyses of the gambler, historian, and birthday celebrant? It is perhaps prudent here to point out first what these achievements of the tragedian do *not* do.

1. They do not render the fated suffering morally dependent on who the hero is.
2. They do not account for the fated suffering by psychological causes. That is, the character of the hero does not in any way bring about or cause his fated suffering.
3. They do not present the inevitability of the tragic fall either as determined by causal accounts or as due to some cosmic fatalism.
4. They do not justify, or attempt to justify, either the suffering of the hero or the paths of fate.

If the tragedian does *not* do these four things, but does do the six things listed earlier, and if the ensuing result is the art form that reveals how we think about fate, then we must ask: What does tragedy reveal about fate? How are we to understand that 'who' the hero is somehow 'illuminates' his suffering? How are we at the same time to deny that 'who' the hero is in any way *causes* or justifies his suffering? And how are we to understand tragic inevitability as somehow grounded in the character (or 'who') of the hero without rendering this a form of predictability? These questions must now be addressed.

6

■   ■   ■

ANALYSIS OF THE
FOUR FIGURES

The preceding discussion of the four figures—the gambler, the historian, the birthday celebrant, and the tragedian— reveals a number of points about our thinking concerning fate and the kindred notions chance, destiny, and fortune. The points are enumerated at the end of each chapter. We must now reflect on the meaning of the four figures. The choice of these figures is based on their *use* of fate or the kindred notions; the discussions are not carried out merely as essays on the different figures for their own sake. We want to know how to think about fate, and the study of these four fated figures will provide important clues or hints as to the inquiry itself.

It should perhaps be reiterated that fate is both a philosophical problem as well as an existential, concrete demand for realization. The haunting image of the goodly woman stricken with a marooning paralysis or the imponderable image of the hapless but worthy youth who draws the shortest straw in the hostage situation cannot ever be entirely forgotten in this study. We are seeking to understand first and foremost how we can *think* about such things without becoming nihilistic or fatalistic. But we also are seeking to find what these ominous possibilities tell us about who we are. Granted, these two questions overlap and perhaps eventually become one question, but the point remains that such fated occurrences seem, at least at first glance, to threaten the very intelligibility of our existence by placing these dread factors beyond the pale of our reason. Their possibility also seems to mock the importance of thought as well as of moral reasoning; for the cruelty of wanton fate not only seems to belittle justice and insult our planning and control but also seems to place the entire range of such influence entirely beyond the limits of our understanding. If we are the playthings of wanton forces, then the lofty status of reason and freedom has been greatly overrated.

But even the cursory examination of the four figures reveals that such misology and despair may not be warranted. To be sure, as we have seen, both the favors and the misfortunes of fate cannot, and should not, be *justified*; but this does not mean they cannot be illuminated, nor does it suggest that what they reveal about who we are need be lamented or despised. The analysis of the four figures constitutes a propaedeutic to the philosophical inquiry; it does not settle or answer sufficiently the leading question "why me?"

One of the most important lessons learned from the study of the four figures is the *difference* between chance, destiny, fortune, and fate. When we think of chance, we seem to appeal merely to the randomness of events, as in the tossing of a coin; and whether this randomness is merely apparent and due to our ignorance or whether there really are gaps in the stern constancy of efficient cause is irrelevant. What emerges from chance is our ability to *play,* and by this delighting in risk we affirm the very wantonness of ungoverned events. Chance makes possible the possible and hence, though uncontrolled, plays a cognitive role. Destiny, however, unfolds our cultural origins in a meaningful though unpredictable way and provides us with the linkage to the past that established our *belonging* to a people. Fortune, celebrated at birthdays, though again ungoverned and uncontrolled, allows us to discover in part who we are by the bestowal of *inheritance.* But it is the tragic artist who ultimately succeeds in showing us how our own existence—the 'who' of our reality—is shaped and formed by a fate rendered *inevitable,* and hence thinkable though not predictable. The distinctions can be characterized as follows: chance gives us *play* (and *risk*); destiny allows us to *belong*; fortune accounts for what we *inherit*; and fate reveals our *meaning.* In seeming opposition to the modalities of our existence that give, bestow, and torment us unjustly are the more revered dimensions of our existence that are favored by those who would make us and our world determinable: knowledge, justice, freedom, and predictability. The four modes of the wanton—chance, destiny, fortune, and fate—seem deeply opposed to the authority and even thinkability of the governed. But analysis of the four figures has shown us that to disjoin the four wantons from the four governing principles is not only overly hasty but also ultimately nihilistic as well. It is not merely that we can courageously *endure* these wanton elements; it is rather that they belong as essential parts of us and, though they cannot be either governed or predicted, are nevertheless intelligible and even worthy of who we are.

It should be pointed out that even the most rigorous of determined disciplines, such as the physical sciences, contain some elements that are not the result of these procedures and are hence beyond the scope of their determination. No causal series is experientially complete, for example, and no scientific system is capable by itself of rendering a complete and coherent metaphysics. Gödel shows us that systems that are complete cannot be consistent, or, if they are consistent, they cannot be complete; Plank's theory of quantum mechanics reveals a certain indeterminacy in the emission of particles; and Heisenberg's "indeterminacy principle" further erodes one's faith in a universe made entirely intelligible solely by reference to mechanistic determinism. Such erosions in no way keep us from relying on the predictability of science, however; they merely show us that science when pressed is not all there is to our powers of understanding.

But even moral reasoning has its limits. As Kant so aptly

puts it, reason may well tell us how we ought to act but cannot guarantee we will do so. If the wicked flourish, then the righteous suffer, and there is no rational principle to set things straight. At the very best we must *postulate* post-terrestial justifying principles that may possibly give us grounds for believing them but certainly contain no necessity for accepting them. Thus, the recognition and awareness that there are limits in the governed disciplines of science and morality in no way render these endeavors less meaningful. At the same time, such awareness should not render us disarmed when we confront the truth of fate, destiny, fortune, and chance. To appeal to these is, therefore, not an appeal to the irrational or to the superstitious. What we must seek are the principles by which one can think about such things as fate and destiny without thereby rendering them justified or determined. And we do this by asking not what causes them or what makes them morally acceptable but what they mean and what light they throw upon the precious mystery of who we are.

But this is to imply that intelligibility is a broader notion than justification or predictability. It is to say that we can think authoritatively about meaning without recourse to determination. In the analysis of two of the four figures, the historian and the tragedian, it may seem that purely aesthetic purposes explain or illuminate this realm of the ungoverned or undetermined. We have seen that through his skill in the unfolding of a people's story the great historian relies upon the notion of destiny to give his narrative a proper sense of direction and inevitability. This thrust of the plot line, destiny, redeems history from being a mere chronicle and keeps us from having to explain momentous events (such as World War I) by an appeal to pathetically insignificant trifles (such as the unworthy Gavrilo Princip). To suggest, however, that because such destiny is revealed only by the historian's pen, and is therefore an ungrounded, subjectivist imposition functioning solely as an aesthetic decoration, is to abuse the power of history. The root of history is truth, not delight, and if aesthetic elements are necessary for the telling of the story, then aesthetics itself is a source of truth and not merely pleasure. Indeed, upon reflection, aesthetics may well be more truthful than science. This is to say the principles of art and beauty, whatever they are, may have greater power in uncovering truth than the mechanistic principles that merely tell us which conditions bring about what effects.

Destiny is thus unfolded only in the telling of the story; it is not discernible in the events themselves. Events in and of themselves are, of course, notoriously unprincipled and uninteresting; it is the interconnection of events that excites our interest. In the model of natural, scientific explanation, this connection is usually thought of as a cause; but in historically significant events, the causes are overshadowed by their seemingly unconnected though hugely pertinent coalescence. We may know what caused Princip to want to kill the Archduke; we may know why the driver mistakenly drove unescorted down Franz-Joseph Street; but why, we ask, did they have to happen at the same time? Coincidence? Possibly, but 'coincidence' is merely the last refuge of a befuddled mind. The point is, when it is told as a story, what seems coincidence on the level of cause becomes destiny on the level of narration. Only a highly arrogant and conceited pedant would insist that the power to give the narration its cohesive force should be excised from the community of reason. Why is empty coincidence somehow more acceptable to the mind than destiny? If, indeed, we are discussing the unfolding truth of our story, coincidence is less revealing than destiny. I no more control coincidence than I do destiny, but the latter is thinkable whereas the former is not. Hence destiny, rather than being a threat to intelligibility, becomes a necessary condition for it in its narrative form. The weaver of the tale must appeal either to coincidence or to destiny, but both are ungoverned. To deny destiny is therefore to eschew not only governance but also intelligibility. Where is the wisdom in this? It is true we cannot control destiny; that is inherent in the meaning of the term. But because we are narratively astute beings, the need for cohesive development of the story line is an essential part of how we make sense of the heritage bestowed by our history. To find this only in the *telling* of the story is a mark not against but for its coherence. Thus merely because destiny relies upon the teller of true tales in no way renders it unworthy of a thoughtful mind.

But fate, as it is revealed in the unfolding of the tragic story, seems less obvious and certainly less concrete. The actions, character, guilt, and genius of George Washington, Thomas Jefferson, or Alexander Hamilton may have coalesced in the original destiny of our nation, but the concrete institution is here and now: I can see it in the political and forensic activity of my daily world, the hideous taxes I pay, the wonderful prejudices of the young about us. But fate is unlike destiny: it is crueler and more terrifying and far, far more random. For the historian has facts to deal with, whereas the tragedian can knit up the craziest of quilts with no regard for accuracy.

The tragedian is so highly indifferent to the morality of his tale that in some tragedies the suffering and grief are entirely undeserved, in others they are entirely deserved, and in still others the audience is unsure. Antigone and Desdemona, for example, do not deserve what happens to them, and desperate attempts by pedants to rake through the texts seeking to unearth a hidden flaw dishonor the plays. Macbeth and Faustus deserve every moment of their anguish; yet this in no way eases the audience of its tragic impact: even with a cruel tyrant like Richard III we simply do not witness his collapse as a lesson in good behavior. Brutus, however, leaves us uneasy about his defeat. The point is simple but irresistible: tragedies cannot be justified morally. The question is not whether their miseries are deserved but whether their miseries eclipse their worth. And the grandeur or nobility of their characters, even when wicked, seems to transcend such grim censure. We leave the theater not feeling sorry for them or even chagrined at their misfortune but instead feeling moved by their nobility.

It is precisely because the noble character of the tragic hero seems the result of the tragedian's skill that we wonder if purely aesthetic factors are at work; but even if they are, this in no way lessens the tragic impact. And it is this impact, so essential for tragedy yet so often dismissed by the theorists, that reveals to us how we think about fate. We have seen this sketched out already in the previous chapter, but now it requires a deeper philosophical analysis.

The impact of tragedy has two origins: the compelling character of the doomed hero and the inevitability of his demise. The character does *not* function as a *cause* of his misfortune either psychologically or morally—a mistake that misled the great Aristotle; nor does the inevitability function as lawlike predictability—a mistake that misled the esteemed Hegel. But, as an impact on the audience, both the character and the inevitability can be seen not only as a philosophical discovery of the highest rank but also as an explanation of the tragic paradox: why we return to the theater.

First we must recognize the nature of the impact. Its impact is truth—not justice, not intellectual satisfaction, not even psychological relief, but a direct and stunning confrontation with truth itself. For tragedy works for one reason only: truth matters. And for truth to matter, who *we* are must matter (hence the importance of character) and who we are must be revealed with the authority or lawlikeness of reason (hence the inevitability).

It must first be seen what is *not* meant by the tragic impact of truth. It does not mean that the tragedian is a shrewd observer of human psychology and thus develops characters so lifelike in their psychological make-up that the audience is moved to applaud the realism of their humanity. Con men and whores probably have sharper eyes for discerning human frailty, and hidden tape recorders of sting operators are far more realistic. Realism, of course, has no place in art, particularly not in poetic or dramatic art; if one wants realism it is better to visit hospitals, sleazy hotels, and prisons than to go to the theater. Truth is not the same as realism. It never ceases to amaze me that energetic critics will praise a vulgar play or film for its being lifelike. In the first place such presentations are 'like' only low-life; and harshness, vulgarity, crudeness, and bad grammar have long since ceased to shock. This is not what is meant by tragedy unfolding the inevitability of truth.

Nor does truth here mean that certain acts must have certain consequences. Indeed, most great tragic plots are so unlikely as to strain our normal credulity. We are not at all inclined to believe that black generals should mistrust their white lieutenants or that wives who lose handkerchiefs will wind up strangled in their beds. Let us leave such dreary predictability to the artless counters of statistics who will never make good playwrights. And finally, tragic truth in no way means accuracy. Julius Caesar simply did not speak as magnificently as Shakespeare has him speak in the play.

What then can it mean to say that the impact of great tragedy lies in the unfolding of truth? Here the probing must be of a most profound philosophical intensity. On its deepest level truth is the arrest of inquiry; it is that which, in stopping us from further inquest, reveals fundamental meaning. Just as the ordinary response to a question stops the interrogation—as the answer "Monday" relieves the question "what day is it?"—so truth in its most original sense brings us to a halt in our fundamental questioning, not by ceasing the inquiry but by enclosing it, thereby giving it legitimacy. By making the torment of the tragic hero too great for success, we are arrested, as a policeman arrests a criminal in flagrante delicto, by the inevitability of existential worth. The truth

simply *stops* our inquisition, our vagueness, our constant pestiferous curiousity and pedantic skepticism with the huge unfolding that we matter. Not that the characters in the play
matter, for they are but mirrors, as Hamlet says, but we the
audience matter. And why do we matter? Because we have
glimpsed the nakedness of truth: suffering, unfairness, injus-
tice cannot eclipse our worth. We matter, not because we are
like Oedipus or Lear but because, as participants in the sacrament of tragedy, we are stunned by unsuccess to the realization that in this sacred rite the enormity of truth stops us
in our tracks, revealing that we are worthy of truth. To behave
in a manner consistent with being worthy of truth is to be
noble. Thus nobility, the loftiest, rarest, and most difficult
virtue to comprehend much less define, is the essential quality of the tragic hero. Without it the plays would not make
tragic sense. The enormous suffering that is undeserved, or if
deserved serves no redemptive purpose, shows us that nobility is independent of success. Fate strips the hero naked; the
garments of success have to be torn from him, for he would
never yield his decency on his own; yet the revealed nakedness is of a vulnerable nobility.

There is a mild but revealing paradox here. The noble
character of the hero is the ground of his fate, but fate must
be ungoverned and undeserved to be tragic. This is because
tragic unsuccess reveals only a worthy nakedness. Not everyone who suffers is noble; not every play with an unhappy ending is a tragedy. The character of Lear does not cause his
daughters to be treacherous; rather it makes his endurance of
the tragedy worthy of witness. The paradox is not why some
men suffer undeservedly but why we want to watch it happen. It is tragedy only when we are compelled to watch it
happen. But why do we watch it at all? Because, stripped of
success, the noble hero shows us the autonomy of his existential worth, and this reveals to us a truth about ourselves *from
which we dare not turn away.*

Beyond the confines of the theater the reality of ungoverned misery is merely endured; within it is fate confronted. For the term 'fate' here does not mean merely the fact that we happen to endure miseries we do not deserve; rather, it entails our embrace of what it means. What does it mean that we are fated? The answer is that our worth cannot be limited to our success. It means we are beings to whom bestowals are essential for who we are. But it also means that the mere fact of undeserved suffering in no way guarantees our existential worth. Ismene is not Antigone. It means, therefore, that truth must matter. Truth, however, is that which *arrests*; it is that beyond which there is no appeal. There can be no truth, then, unless there is the possibility of affirming that beyond which there is no appeal; and the noble endurance of the cruelties of chance, destiny, and fortune is beyond appeal. This is fate.

But if nobility, conceived as that which makes us worthy of truth, explains the *character*, we still need to explore the dimension of *inevitability*. What is inevitable, we say, *must* happen. But this necessity is of various sorts: there is logical necessity, which simply means that the consequent is formally contained in the antecedent; there is natural necessity, which means that certain events always cause other events and hence is the same as predictability; there is moral necessity, by which we mean one has certain duties and obligations that ought to be performed; and finally there is tragic inevitability, which means that the sorry end of the story is uniquely fitting, that no other ending serves as well to provide the impact of truth.

This deserves our reflection. In the final act of *King Lear*, the dying Edmund, slain by his noble brother Edgar, dispatches a messenger to interdict the bastard's death warrant on Lear and Cordelia. Albany is moved to shout one of the most revealing lines of the play: "Run, Run, oh run!" (V, 3).

For, were the messenger to achieve his task and arrive at the prison *on time,* the play would end in glorious triumph. We ache to see this accomplished. Little wonder that Nahum Tate simply gives us a fleeter messenger in his adaptation of *Lear* and all is then well.

There is no logical prohibition against the messenger having quicker feet. Nor are there physical reasons that would impede his success. Certainly there are no moral reasons, for justice and right screech and howl that the messenger should get there on time. King Lear would still be King Lear if the execution were avoided: we know this because Nahum Tate did write an acceptable play in which the messenger arrived on time, and the entire eighteenth century was glad of it.

Perhaps, though, King Lear would not have been King Lear had the messenger arrived on time. The play certainly would not have been *King Lear.* For who else is King Lear except he who is so nakedly revealed as one defeated by fortune, denuded by a cruel mischance on which so much salvation depends? Were Cordelia not to have died, we, the audience, who alone matter in the theater, would be cheated of something we have earned by the anguish of the first four acts: the full measure of who Lear is, which is the unfolding of Lear's fate. It is the rightful ending, the true ending, because it provides the narrative inevitability that makes tragedy true rather than merely entertaining.

We all must die. But some die out of season; some die in a manner entirely disconnected with how they live. This is actuality. But even in actuality there are some whose very deaths seem to befit their lives: a peaceful, gentle woman dying gently and peacefully in her granddaughter's bed; a violent, fiery youth dying courageously in a sacrificial act of daring. They died as they lived and we find this curiously fitting. But in art, which mirrors reality, not actuality, and hence truth rather than fact, only the most skilled writers can so wreak a character as to plant in us the powerful sense of impending necessity with which the destined doom flows on the current of an aesthetic logic. We see the death of the tragic hero as a source of illumination on his life, and that just makes the seeming randomness of chance events *thinkable* rather than merely *noticeable*. For I *note* things that happen, but I *think* things that must happen.

But what does this tell us about fate? That we can think about it rather than just note it? This seems to contradict the very meaning of fate, which is that we cannot understand or govern or control its power. How are we to make sense of this?

In this present reflection we have focused on the tragedian, and to a lesser extent on the historian, whose skill in weaving stories provides us with a narrative cohesion that makes either fate or destiny seem intelligible. In both cases the sense of inevitability occurs after the telling and not before, so it is not predictable, like science. But whether before or after, the coherence between antecedent and consequent is there and hence is rendered thinkable. But in the case of the gambler's chance or the birthday celebrant's fortune there is no transcendent storyteller. Chance, in order to *be* chance, must be entirely random and not grounded in the character of the dice thrower. The infant is born of this man and that woman, with absolutely no say in the matter and no designing artisan to make this random mixing of genes more rational than any other. To overlook the randomness of fate and overstress the inevitability of it seem unwarranted and misguided.

But the audience and the playwright do not deny the random. Indeed the greatest of them seem to revel in it. The trivialities, whether the slowness of messengers or the accidental dropping of handkerchiefs, are meant not to diminish our worth but to enhance it. For the play shows that what really matters outlasts and outranks these lethal minutiae of everyday life. It is not that Romeo's or Cordelia's life would have been spared had the messengers been more swift that matters; what matters is the nobility of their confrontation of their fate, which is *causally* random but *existentially* inevitable. And it is this difference, this triumph of the existentially significant *over* the causally random, that prepares us for the awesome confrontation of truth that fate, when properly understood, provides.

This fate has two contrasting but synthesizing modalities that make it significant. It is, as we learn from the gambler and the birthday celebrant, entirely unpredictable, wanton, ungoverned, and thus apparently incapable of being thought about. Yet it is manifested in the works of tragedians and historians as narratively inevitable, though not causally predictable, hence apparently capable of being thought about. From the gambler's perception of the sheer wantonness of chance, however, we also discover that a world with *no* random elements, a world entirely governed by logical, physical, or moral necessity, is a world entirely lacking in grace, forgiveness, and play. Finite reason, *being* finite, celebrates this randomness in bestowing, forgiving, and above all playing. But finite reason, being *reason*, must have its lawlike linkage; hence the historian and tragedian provide us with narrative inevitability. The purely random cannot be thought, and so we need the storyteller to *show* us the weave of destiny and fate grounded in character; the entirely nonrandom cannot be endured, and so we need the player and the celebrant to *show* us how to affirm these gaps in the grim thrust of law.

The analyses of the four figures, however, seem to be designed to make fate not only intelligible, if only indirectly, but also affirmable. That is, I cannot only *think* about fate, I can also be glad there is fate, even if it entails unwarranted suffering. This, however, is only the first face of fate. There is another side.

PART THREE

FATE

AS

ABANDONMENT

■ ■ ■

CHAPTER

7

. . .

ABANDONMENT

It is as if they whom we honor and love, whose favor and esteem provide confidence and devotion, have in a gesture entirely bereft of reason turned their backs on us, as if we were spotted children discarded on the grass. We are forgotten. Our exchequer is forfeit, our names excised from the precious lists, our places at the table removed. There is no memory of us. They among the radiant do not recall who we are or that we ever were. We are but gaps in the line where once we proudly stood; and we do not know why. We are abandoned.

Abandonment has left us unremembered and uncounted. To think about this supreme forgetting seems beyond our powers, for to think requires a home, and we have lost the key. Unranked we can demand no redress; disowned we can entreat no kinship; unjudged we can submit no plea. Our anguish evokes no pity, our absence no remorse. Forgotten, but why? Rejected, for what reason? Marooned, for what offense? We ask, but none will hear. We entreat, but none respond. Yet this is neither hell nor banishment, neither prison nor exile. It is but fated existence. For fate is the cruelest power: it is indifference. We ask "why me?" and hear the mocking echo "who cares?"

To be fated is to be left to capricious fortune, to be abandoned to indifference; and indifference is, by its very meaning, impervious to reason, to outrage, and to judgment. It is the curse of all, and perhaps even more so for those who are seemingly blessed by fleeting favor, for their cheerful distraction with their own petty success merely blinds them to this dread truth. To be fated is not to count; but to be cheerfully unaware is not only to be irrelevant but also to be beguiled. For if our fortunes and our destiny are determined by indifferent powers, then we are cheated of all legitimacy; our continued presence is an embarrassment. To speak of fate is to deny sense to our existence, not in the nihilistic disregard for reason but in the hideous awareness that though there *are* reason, right, goodness, justice, and honor, they do not apply to *us*, for we are abandoned.

To be abandoned means to be left out, forgotten. It means not that there is no home but simply that the door is closed to us. We are capable of reason, but if the world itself is unreasonable, then this capacity for governed thinking dislocates who we are. We rely on cause, we arrange our environment to our advantage, we discover from our own minds the rules of good conduct and how to achieve esteem, we are purposive and so we propose good and decent things using the technological skill to carry them out. And the entire enterprise then is sabotaged by some fly's wing, a tiny insignificant trifle that sets awry the entire machinery of reasoned effort, mocking all that is sane with the grain of insanity. How many lofty towers have fallen to an ungoverned flaw in the fundamental stone? If an unlucky turn down Franz-Josef Street wreaks the devastation of an entire culture and continent, then the world is unreasoned and we reasoners do not belong. We have lost our place in it. The world abandons us.

For to be fated seems an assault against our status as free and rational beings. But if it is reason itself that has confronted us with this bleak prognosis, then we are abandoned by it. For reason in its most critical moment has left us, bereft of its protection, to the stings and assaults by ungoverned gremlins, which the solemn assure us simply must be endured.

To recognize that we are fated is to accept perforce being abandoned, because, in the realization that all is not governed or controllable, perhaps not even rational, there is more than the cognitive awareness of our limits. There is also the inevitable realization that this situation leaves us somehow incomplete or lost. Things are not quite as they should be. Indeed things seem on the very brink of ribald silliness and nonsense. We are abandoned not only by the world but also by reason itself.

When the lover is abandoned by his beloved, the distraught suitor is not merely wretched because he has forfeited all joy; he senses rather that his own worth has been rendered a casual and mocked plaything, where so recently it was esteemed and vital. His power to illuminate has been unsocketed from the only lamp worth glowing. Abandonment is thus mockery of one's own worth, for it surrenders the very thinkability of our worth over to the incidental, the dismissable, the replaceable. We would rather endure almost any torment than this, for torments can ennoble the endurance and sanction the effort. But abandonment rejects utterly. Even the punished fare better, for they are respected in their suffering as morally significant; but where is the significance at all for the forgotten?

Thrown into this fearsome silence and limitless emptiness, what can we do? We make noise to dispel the deafening hush, we distract ourselves with silliness, being deprived of the serious. We make playful the macabre in an attempt to resurrect the sanctioned; we roar and rage against ourselves in pale imitation of being roared against by those who no longer care; we seek distraction lest we be distracted. But in these pale and petty efforts we only deceive ourselves. We bang tin cans and empty pots to ward off a silence heavy with truth, and the noise is the illusion. And we know it. Thus we mock ourselves. Perhaps there is nothing left but to lament, to pity ourselves for what we somehow lost without knowing why. The orphans weep, not in expectation of comfort but simply at the dreadful plight of being orphaned. It is without hope. It is despair. It is the end of sense and reason.

Yet, though these analyses are true and valid, thinkers do not crawl into some nihilistic hole and gnash their teeth, seeking redress in pitiable lamentation. Perhaps we simply should not probe this deeply. Fate is rarely analyzed to any great depth by most philosophers, and the reason may be that the dark truth that awaits these researches is simply unworthy of the digging. Men do not risk their lives in dripping mines searching for sand; the end result is not worth the effort. So perhaps thinkers should simply leave the fate question unasked, for the truth discovered is simply too bleak to warrant the search. If our inquiry reveals the inevitability of abandonment by both reason and the world, then perhaps, like the sacred mysteries of some Levantine religion, it should simply not be broached.

The inquiry does indeed reveal our fundamental abandonment. But its revelation is truth, and that is the mother vein for the digger, so we cannot abandon it merely because it abandons us. Are we then left to self-pity, weeping as the orphan weeps simply because of who we are? But this, we say, is unworthy of us. Self-pity forfeits all respect; it is a whine whose discordant jarring sets our teeth on edge and moves us to remove. To yield to self-pity is not befitting a human being.

But here is a discordant note that demands the offending string be retuned. To say that self-pity is unworthy of us is to assume our worth in some way. If we were entirely unworthy, this capitulation to the base whine of pity would be of no matter; but it is. And so we must strum the chord again to see which jangling string is out of tune.

The truth, however, remains. Fate cannot be justified; and in its rebellion against the hegemony of order and reason, and in our awareness of fate, we become aware of our abandonment. The stern warrant of truth arrests us here, and we cannot avoid the indictment. But we can yield neither to the shrinking power of pity nor to the misological appeal to limiting inquiry.

What has the argument shown? We are reasoners; the world has revealed itself in chance, destiny, fortune, and fate as unjustified. Hence we have lost our place in the world; that is, we are abandoned. Being reasonable, the unreasonable world cannot provide us with our home, so we are outcasts and orphans. Because it is reason that brings us to this realization, we are abandoned by our most dear and precious aspect. So why not take comfort either in refusing to inquire this deeply or in the truth-eclipsing whine of self-pity? What allegiance do we, the abandoned, have to the unsmiling, unfavoring sovereignty of truth? None. So let us pity ourselves, and our whines will rail against the impotent regent.

It is not because we do not like pity; that is an empirical matter. It is, as we moderns quaintly say, up to the consumer. It is rather that self-pity exacerbates the very pain that calls forth the mewing in the first place. Self-pity simply makes us all the more pitiable. And putting a limit on our search for truth, placing the quest for fate beyond our inquiry, changes truth to deception. It is not a moral matter or a matter of character; it is simply unavoidable, like fate itself. We cannot escape through these deceptions. Our backs are perhaps up against the wall, and we must confront whatever is hunting us down.

Fate ceases to be fate if it is justified. But justification is not the same as illumination. The reality of abandonment cannot be avoided, but neither can it reduce us to disarmed whiners. Indeed it is in the very reality, the very *truth* of abandonment that we can find illumination.

Unlike the first four figures, this analysis will not show us the benefits to chance, destiny, fortune, and fate; rather, only in showing that fate does indeed render us abandoned can we learn its truth that has no benefit and hence is truth in its purest sense.

To imply that fate is irrational because it cannot be justified is an overly narrow view of reason. It suggests that reason's role in the endurance of undeserved misfortune is limited to justifying our suffering. Obviously reason cannot render un-justified suffering justified; but that does not remove reason entirely from this grim truth. To argue that unjustified suffer-ing is self-contradictory assumes that some principle is vio-lated when bad luck comes our way. But what is the source of this principle? There seems to be no compelling reason to believe that rationality must guarantee success. But the critic may protest that it is not the suffering caused by misfortune that is undeserved but simply that, being undeserved, it seems to render our existence unintelligible; that is, the fate of the fortunate and the fate of the wretched are equally in-telligible simply because both are unanswerable. But this renders the meaningfulness of existence unthinkable.

It may render the meaning of existence unjustifiable, that is, it may show us we cannot determine why one should en-dure bad luck whereas another should be blessed with good luck, but these uneven assignments of fortune are not thereby contradictory. This requires a deeper probing.

It has been shown that undeserved misfortune entails a sense of abandonment in which we, as rational, are aliens in an irrational universe. There is no attempt here to deny that an effect of this sort results in abandonment; rather what must be denied is that this abandonment is unthinkable or irratio-nal. In order to show that this is not so, we must look more closely at the presuppositions that lie at the basis of the nihil-istic claim.

The model assumed in this argument is that the rational

subject is entirely disjoined from the random, and hence irrational, world. The world, we say, may be rational in terms of natural events, that is, every event does have a cause, but it is not rational in the moral sense of people being treated fairly; there seems to be no *reason* to explain why one is favored and another abused by fortune. Thus we distinguish meaningful subjects, that is, rational and responsible people, from a meaningless world in which these meaningful subjects live. The world may be rational in a scientific sense but meaningless in an existential sense. The term 'fate' refers to this noncorrespondence.

But the flaw in the above paragraph is revealed upon more serious reflection. First, there cannot be such a severe disjunction between 'subject' and 'world'. Every subject is already in the world, and every use of the term or notion 'world' must presuppose a rational subject. For I am not first a worldless entity that is then somehow placed in an alien world; rather my existence as such is intelligible only because I am *already* in the world. The philosopher may even characterize this necessity of being in the world as a priori. That is, to think about myself as meaningful *must* be to think about myself as in the world. To be meaningful is to be in the world. But if by the term 'world' we mean that ultimate source that provides us with a dwelling, and if this world is characterized by indifference or indeterminacy as to the bestowals of fortune, then no formal violation of either moral or ontological reasoning is involved. To be is to be in the world (this is *necessarily* so), but to be in the world is to be bestowed by ungoverned fortune. Where is the irrationality in this? It would *perhaps* be *preferable* to be in a world in which all pleasure and pain were simply deserved, but it cannot be logically required. It cannot even be morally required, since morality assumes a responsible agent, and the world would have to be a conscious and free agent in its bestowals of good and bad fortunes. Of course, if good and bad fortunes were indeed based on moral deserving they would be neither bestowals nor fortunes. So what the critical protest really demands is that all bestowals and all fortune are self-contradictory notions. This cannot be shown.

Second, what does 'world' mean outside our existential involvement in it? Or does it *have* a meaning except as the dwelling place for conscious, meaningful beings? Just as there can be no 'mind' without the world for the mind to be in, so there can be no world independent of our minds. This is not to say that entities within the world depend for their existence on our minds; it is to say that the term 'world' is a meaningful term only if we dwell in it. Although formal logicians like to talk about 'possible worlds', there really cannot be a plurality of worlds, possible or actual. We exist in the world, and whatever meaning can be extracted from this modality that can be designated as 'world' is all there is to the world. The world cannot be an independent thing-out-there, as are sea-shells and wooden shoes, for all things are already in the world, and the world cannot be in itself. This means that my being in the world is fated, not that the world, conceived somehow independently of my being in it, is random. To conceive of the world as externality is to conceive of it as entirely governed, that is, as nature. What is random is not nature but the existential meaning given to the realization that I can neither discern nor control why I should be victimized by chance events. It is therefore not the *world* that is random but my *being* in the world that is subject to randomness. In other words, the abandonment is not from an indifferent world to a reasoning subject but from being in the world as dweller to being in the world as alien. The difference is solely in the ways or modes in which I exist *as* being in the world. I am not forgotten *by* the world but rather abandoned in my own way of being in the world. How is this possible?

To illuminate the meaning of fate, rather than to justify it, requires that it be seen in terms of our own existence instead of in terms of the external world's indifference to our concerns. What the intelligibility of our own existence reveals is, therefore, the focus of the inquiry; and because we are indeed abandoned by the cruelty of fate, this can only mean that our existence itself is made intelligible by the conflict between our being controlled and controlling on the one hand and our being random and ungoverned on the other.

That is, fate is due not to the gap between a mindless world and a meaningful thinker but to two internal and conflicting modalities within *us*. Fate is not external but internal to us; and the conflict of abandonment is precisely that in us between what is given or bestowed and what is earned or deserved. To be able to dwell is meaningful only if one is also able to be abandoned: they are conflicting but correlative terms, or disjuncts, necessary for the very intelligibility of existence. Just as 'good' and 'bad' are both necessary for ethics and 'large' and 'small' both necessary for measuring, so 'alien' and 'akin' are necessary to think about being in the world, for this "in" is either 'dwelling', in which we *belong* in the world, or 'abandoned', in which we are banished in it. Thus, the 'in' is understood not in a physical, geographical sense but in the existential sense of what is presupposed in order to make our being in the world intelligible, that is, capable of being *thought* about. To be in the world thus can be either as dwellers or as abandoned, or can even be a combination: somewhat as dweller and somewhat as abandoned. Being 'abandoned' does not mean existing entirely outside the world but simply existing *as* one who is understood, in part, as the recipient of the undeserved, whether good or bad. Abandonment is realized when this modality waxes negatively beyond our comprehension. Yet we may at times feel hugely favored when chance bestows good fortune, at which time we may well feel very privileged to be in the world of bestowal, that is, in the world made sense of by recognizing the bestowing modality. We cannot, however, make a simplistic equation of abandonment with bestowal and belonging with control. For we are always both responsible and at the same time vulnerable to the ungoverned, whether abandoned or belonging.

Thus it is not necessary to appeal to erratic or irrational forces in the world to account for fate; rather we must seek its meaning in the way our existence becomes intelligible to us, namely, that we are both governor and victim, that we plan and sometimes succeed because of our planning, but that we sometimes fail in spite of it due to random events. We are thrown as inheritors and we are thoughtfully responsible, but in either case or both we are still always in the world.

To dwell in the world and to be alien in the world are fundamental ways we exist. To be abandoned is therefore *not* to be rational in an irrational world but to be able to lose our way because we are not complete masters of all that happens.

Let us look more closely at the cruel abandonment of the lover. She did love him; he still loves her. But she now no longer loves him. He is aware that "these things happen"; that is, we do not control them. He also knows that, as unmarried, there is no legal or contractual obligation on her part to remain with him. Yet, rejected by this dominant passion, he feels abandoned not only by *her* but by the *world*. The reason for this is because he realizes that her loving him earlier and her not loving him now were not the result of rational calculation; his being loved by her was just as unpredictable and unaccountable as her falling out of love with him, so he does not blame her. But his anguish is real. The world seems not only an alien place but even a hostile one. He no more deserves his present suffering than he deserved his earlier joy; but to be rejected by a former lover who is still beloved is to endure the dread diminution of worth, the belittling of one's importance that is abandonment. This is not merely bad luck, it is bad existence; the very *meaning* of existence seems darkened, foreign, abstract, and uninteresting. And, most importantly, we cannot understand it; we do not know why it happens. But this lack of understanding is revealed as essential to the way in which we exist. Hence, though it is not understandable as to causes and not even acceptable to us in terms of our preference, it is not logically inconsistent with our understanding of who we are. For a robust and healthy person the anguish may not be as lasting as the cruelty of a life-long paralysis or even as shocking as a youthful death, but that it leaves us, even temporarily, out of sync or alienated cannot be avoided or denied.

What matters, of course, is not how one *feels*, for that may differ from person to person, but that the philosophical location of the inquiry has been profoundly altered. Fate ceases to be a cosmological or even metaphysical problem and becomes instead an existential matter available for philosophical analysis. One must focus on the concrete, existential reality of *being* abandoned, not merely of *feeling* abandoned, and discover from this analysis the ontological presuppositions— that is, what I *first* must assume as true about who I am or what it means for me to exist at all—in order to make sense of what it means to be abandoned.

We have discovered that to be abandoned means to suffer a diminution of worth due to the alienation of self from self, that is, myself as worthy because of my own deserving and myself as worthy because of what is bestowed. Abandonment adjusts the tuner so as to render the bestowed meaning entirely out of focus with the earned meaning, and as a consequence not only is my worth diminished but my attunement is rendered out of focus: I no longer *belong* with myself.

It must be reiterated that this cannot be justified or even ameliorated by psychological pep talks. For some, the psychological effects and ramifications of this are devastating, perhaps even fatal. Any attempt to belittle or to diminish the wrenching anguish of abandonment is simply unworthy of respect. But the point is one not of despair or hope but of thought. Fate, in its cruel manifestation in our being abandoned, nevertheless reveals. What it reveals is truth, and in particular truth about how we are to think of our existence, namely, as fundamentally tensed between control and victim. This inquiry will show that the worth of this truth is beyond all else and hence transcends all lesser concerns. But before this can be shown, it is necessary to consider, and ultimately reject, various nonexistential attempts to explain this inescapable phenomenon. The purpose of these critical reflections is not merely to show the inadequacy of unsuccessful theories, for that is pedantry, but to learn greatly from theories, which, though ultimately lacking, are by no means unworthy of serious analysis. The reality and inescapability of fate have been with us for as long as human history has been blessed with reflection, and there is too much wisdom in these profound probings to warrant their dismissal without first examining them with respect. And like the gold-hungry prospector, we must wash the gravel and sluice the sand to find the glittering dust even in a humble stream. There are three attempts to account for fated abandonment that deserve to be analyzed: the first is the purely natural account that appeals to the principle that nature respects species and not individuals; the second is the stoic account that finds in moral endurance an ennobling virtue; and the third and by far the most compelling is that of the theodicist, who endeavors to give theological justification to the seemingly wanton selections of cruelty. Only after these three profound but finally misleading accounts are confronted can the inquiry proceed to the final considerations.

CHAPTER

8
▪ ▪ ▪

THE THREE
JUSTIFICATIONS

NATURE

Nature, they say, does not respect individuals, only species.
The male lion will kill the suckling cubs of a female whom he
has achieved by right of victorious combat over the cubs' sire,
and the female will submit to the advances of the new dominant male of the pride. This seems cruel, but if the species is
to flourish the individuals must be sacrificed. Some species
produce many offspring because their predators are ubiqui-
tous and powerful: the species succeeds through sheer number. The insect world is replete with females who kill their
mate once his function has been fulfilled. The zoologists can
tell us countless stories in the animal kingdom in which nature manifests this Jovian indifference to the plight of the one
when the menace is to the many.

This also is true, though with ramifications, of the human
species, as when the sacrifice of the few valiant men of the
Royal Air Force in saving Britain is honored with great ora-
tory. In these cases, of course, the sacrifice is freely made,
but the idea of the one or the few suffering or dying for the
sake of the many is incorporated into our understanding. Nature seems indifferent to who we are, to our private wants,

needs, and worth; it is how we fit into the grander scheme and purpose of the race that seems to matter.

These examples from nature, however, merely state the fact. But facts alone, even those that seem to disclose the maxims by which the biological sciences are governed, do not and cannot justify the seeming misology—if not nihilism—entailed in this wanton disregard for private significance. What comfort is there for the mangled lion cub in the realization that now the strongest male will breed half-brothers with his own mother, thereby preserving the species? When a leopard brings down an impala with ruthless savagery, where is the evil? Were the leopard to fail in this, both she and her young would starve; when she is successful, the impala is killed and her young left motherless. So nature demands cruelty. Yet none call it evil or wicked. Indeed we understand that this is the way things are supposed to happen in nature. It is nature's way.

It is not these natural phenomena that offend; but it is the appeal to the preference of the species over the individual as a justification for undeserved suffering that is unacceptable. I should like to designate this way of thinking as the 'Bambi fallacy', with all due apologies to the genius of Walt Disney. *Bambi* is a brilliant film, deserving of its honors and accolades, and children as well as adults will forever enjoy its beauty and power. But there is, nevertheless, even about this masterpiece a point that needs to be made (though only a most malicious ogre would ever dare to defame the wondrous innocence of *Bambi*).

In the film the fantasized life of a deer named Bambi is depicted, first in his youthful and charming innocence as a fawn; then in his humorous bewilderment as a four-legged adolescent falling in love with Faleen, the local teen-age doe; and finally as an emerging, adult stag, complete with a magnificent multitined display of kingly antlers. When Bambi is born the other forest creatures call him the "young prince,"

THE THREE JUSTIFICATIONS • 135

for Bambi's father, called the "great prince," is a mighty stag, imperiously watching over the entire forest from a lofty crag. On occasion this mighty stag descends his high crest to lead Bambi safely from peril, which appears in the form of hunters, fierce dogs, and even a forest fire. After Bambi matures and woos the lovely Faleen, their union produces offspring, twins as lovable as their father had been. But now Bambi himself stands majestically on the tor by his father's side. As the film ends, the old, wise, noble stag slowly turns and leaves Bambi alone on the cliff's edge, apparently to rule now in his father's place, no longer the "little prince" but the new "great prince," lord of the forest and its beloved denizens.

Even a child cannot miss the point. This is a circle. Bambi's child will have the same wonderful experiences; one day Bambi too will die, and though we shed a tear, perhaps, his son will occupy the tor and life will go on. For in the last analysis, it is the unfolding of the eternal circle of life that is important; it lasts forever, whereas the fleeting, ephemeral existence of the single deer—or person—is naught but the servitor of this wondrous cycle.

Is there comfort in this? Indeed there is. The tear is shed only because we have given this one deer a name, Bambi. The message is clear: it is the cycle that matters. The death of the noble stag deflects us only briefly; nature is fecund and resilient, but, above all, nature is everlasting. We take comfort in belonging to this grander order, and it is a peculiarity of children that their vulnerability and innocence in which the future is preciously locked seek comfort in belonging. Children are fundamentally familial beings, and when the whole forest, which mirrors the whole world, is shown as *theirs*, a place where they are able to resist all the ravages of fires and evil hunters, the comfort is palpable. It is even presented as justificatory. The aged yield gracefully to the younger powers, which is as it ought to be. The individual yields to the larger process, which is as it ought to be. Even death serves its purpose: to make room for the new. The departure of the old stag, replaced with the new great prince, Bambi, is absorbed by the wider story and hence is justified. Knowing that we *belong* to the greater family, our lives, even our misfortunes, are justified.

But what is curiously left out of Bambi's story is Bambi. For, if the story works, Bambi is replaceable. Though this is comfort, it is comfort at a price. Indeed, the price is terrible. For we have been deceived. We thought, as the film unwinds, that we were growing fond of this deer named Bambi, but our affections are obviously fickle, for when the new fawn is born and Bambi removes to the towering crag, we discover it is not Bambi we loved at all but simply *any* fawn as cute and lovable as the Disney artists can create. It is not even *this* deer replaced with *that* deer that we apparently hold dear; it is the *replacing* that matters. We take comfort in being replaceable.

This is not deception. The fact is that there can indeed be considerable solace found in belonging to a process, a movement, a reality that transcends the brevity of our own, private existence. Men and women take authentic and genuine comfort in the thought that their children will continue the line of their forefathers; heroes of various sacrificial deaths have smiled as they expire, knowing that what is of their own can now continue. This is not only solace but also a justification in a sense. For our existence is *not* merely a private affair; who we are, as we have seen in the previous chapters, cannot be disjoined from those with whom we share our lives or from where we dwell. Since our family is a part of us, there is some justification in recognizing that our worth is not entirely eclipsed as long as some remain.

The impala devoured by the hungry leopard serves a purpose as the sacrificed hero serves a purpose. If the laws of nature seem to render inevitable chance misfortunes, then that this man or that woman must endure them is to some extent justified, because what matters is not this or that person but humanity as a whole, for humanity is *in* this world of chance and mischance.

But the Bambi fallacy is sinister; for in "justifying" the suffering of undeserved misfortune of the one by showing how it fits into nature's scheme is to forfeit entirely all existential worth. If indeed nature is the only explanation, then there is no fate at all. For fate becomes nothing other than the principle of indifference to individuals. To say that nature is "indifferent" to whether the leopard goes hungry or the impala is devoured is simply to say that we are restricted to understanding only the broader principles, that there *are no* principles that can illuminate how to think about *this* leopard's hunger or *that* impala's terror. The Bambi fallacy merely reiterates abandonment; it does not justify it. For the defeated impala or the hapless child who wanders on the leopard-infested veldt, there is no justification or reason. It is simply bad luck, and the impala, the leopard, and the child are abandoned totally. We simply do not and cannot *think* about them, for there are no principles available to think *with,* and hence the Bambi fallacy abandons them as cruelly as any human indifference.

This is not a fault of naturalistic explanations; it is merely the realization of their limits. The outrage is that some would have us appeal to the Bambi fallacy as a source of solace or explanation. As charming as the story is, it contains a vicious cruelty underneath, for it not only shows that in nature there is no respect for individuals but also communicates this indifference as a justification to the young and impressionable.

STOICISM

From the film *Bambi* we can now turn to an incident in Shakespeare's *Julius Caesar,* in which Portia, Brutus's wife, stabs herself in the leg to show her stoic endurance and thereby to become worthy of her husband's trust. Portia's act

seems remarkable if not downright perverse to our modern
hedonistic tendencies, but there can be no doubt that stoicism, in some guise or other, offers attractive alternatives to
either the simple nihilism of rejection or the deceptive allure
of the Bambi fallacy. For the stoics, pain, particularly undeserved or unwarranted pain, provides an essential distancing
mechanism by which one separates the spiritual realm from
the physical or animalistic realms. By the distancing, the nobility of the individual character is not only revealed but actually achieved. That is, Portia not only *shows* her husband
that she has Roman strength but also, through her self-
induced act of pain, wins a victory over the baser instincts,
thereby *making* her trustworthy. Stoic endurance is hence not
a causal but a moral appeal. It does not question why the
undeserved pain selects a specific sufferer but simply argues
that in enduring it with dignity we achieve a higher, morally
superior, level of existence.

True moral stoicism must be distinguished from sado-
masochistic perversion. The stoic sufferer does not take un-
natural pleasure from his pain. Rather, in suffering and
enduring the pain, he sees it as an opportunity for achieving
moral superiority. He cannot become physically indifferent to
the pain, but he can become morally impervious to its effects.
Thus, the stoic can indeed *justify* pain as a means to achieving
moral worth. If one inserts a further belief in some post-
terrestial reward, the endurance of the pain may even be seen
as a personal benefit; but stoicism generally seems to offer
special pride in eschewing these appeals to calculative advantage.

The radical stoic who makes the positive, metaphysical assertion that pain is itself good on the basis of this strengthening effect of undeserved suffering on the character is of course
making an invalid inference. What is good is the strengthened
character, not the pain itself. It may indeed be morally superior to endure pain without complaint, but it cannot simply

be morally good to have pain. Crime provides an opportunity to allow the institutions of justice to go to work, but this does not make crime itself good. The stoic's admirable concern with strengthening his character may show that unwanted and unwarranted suffering need not defeat us because our moral worth is independent of our bodily satisfactions. In this the stoic has justified his endurance, not the fates themselves. Should the stoic take the next step and argue that undeserved suffering is really a benefit, then he is no longer a stoic but a theodicist.

The stoic, therefore, is fundamentally appealing because he *distracts* us from the question of fate. By disregarding entirely the ontological and metaphysical wonder about why this man or that woman should be chosen by random fortune, the stoic draws our attention solely to the point of character. From an indifferent fate randomly selecting its victims, the indifferent sufferer shrugs off the question as irrelevant, so that random indifference of chance is countered and defeated by the grander indifference of the morally autonomous. But though this may be admirable, it is not illuminating. The victim of random suffering may well endure his pain nobly and by this achieve a strengthening of character; but he may still want to know why he was selected. He may even be glad he was selected because of the opportunity it offers to allow him to grow spiritually, but his subsequent indifference to the questions of whence and why is not philosophically helpful. For in the last analysis, even if we are made better by enduring it, we still would like to know how to think about the seeming random selection. Even if it makes me better, I want to know "why me?" and if the stoic answer is "because it makes you better" I am distracted rather than enlightened. What makes me better by enduring fortune nobly is not fortune but me.

If one examines the argument of the stoics along with the presuppositions, the persuasive impact is impressive; but it is impressive precisely because it distracts from the principle of fate. The argument deserves to be traced.

1. Pain cannot be seen as bad. For if the pain is *deserved*, then in enduring it justice is served. If the pain is *undeserved*, then the enduring of it broadens the gap between the base and the noble within the soul of the sufferer.
2. The presupposition that must be assumed if this argument is to be persuasive is that our moral worth consists in our triumph over our baser instincts.
3. But unless this triumph *is* what makes us noble, we are victims of wanton forces like fate.
4. To admit to this kind of slavery is to be debased.
5. Thus, indifference, sometimes amounting to disdain, to the significance and importance of these chance misfortunes becomes a necessary quality for achieving independence from them. I cannot avoid being a victim of chance misfortune, but I can avoid letting it matter.
6. Therefore, to achieve greatness of spirit and the pinnacle of moral worth, fate must be disregarded entirely. For it is not the randomness of the pain that matters but the effect of the pain: the divorce of spirit from the influence of the baser instincts, desire for pleasure, and avoidance of pain.

Whether this argument entails the metaphysical claim that one is possessed of a body that is base and a soul that is noble is both moot and irrelevant. For the *fact* cannot be denied: some men are capable of enduring pain nobly, and the *nobility* of this endurance cannot be denied even if the metaphysical entity called 'soul' can be denied. Indeed it may even be nobler to endure the pain without asking for the metaphysical justification.

As splendid as this may seem, however, it places the highest achievement of moral worth as an impediment to truth. For one's moral perfection may be achieved at the sacrifice of the more radiant virtue, which is the realization that truth matters. Self-knowledge is also a virtue, and if the stoic endurance of pain accomplishes an indifference to our being fated, then moral worth and the worth of truth are put in opposition. The questionable step in the argument is thus identified as (2). Is nobility *merely* the triumph over the baser instincts; or is a profound awe toward truth the deeper meaning to nobility? And can truth be honored if the achievement of moral worth depends on an indifference to who we are?

The point remains, however, that it is not pain but the heroic endurance of it that elevates the soul. To a weaker person than the stoic hero, pain may well reduce the sufferer to despair, and hence the mere possibility of heroic endurance does not justify pain. Further, it is not enough *merely* to endure pain in order to achieve nobility. Kant, who often sounds rather like a stoic, insists that such endurance may well lift us out of the baser reliance on the lower sentiments but nevertheless adds that such endurance is in itself unworthy unless it is endured for the right reason: because it is one's duty. But this Kantian refinement, though perhaps more insightful, distracts from the pristine purity of the stoic sufferer.

Thus stoicism, like the naturalist account and the Bambi fallacy, attempts to justify the wanton misfortunes of chance and fate by pointing to the ennobling effect that the endurance of these barbs has on the soul. This is accomplished by an artificially induced indifference to our vulnerability to fate and hence distracts us from a confrontation with the truth of our being fated. This, and the realization that it is not fate itself but simply the endurance of it that justifies, shows the limits of this remarkable imperium of character over misfortune. Like the naturalist, the stoic indeed justifies, but at a price—the worth of truth—and hence suffers, as does the naturalist, by failing to illuminate.

THEODICY

From nature and stoicism we now turn to theodicy, as exemplified in John Milton's great epic *Paradise Lost*:

> That, to the height of this great argument
> I may assert Eternal Providence,
> And justify the ways of God to men.
>
> (I, 24)

Milton is not the first to try to do this, but as a theodicist he and the philosopher Leibniz are unparalleled. The term 'theodicy', from the two Greek words θεος 'god' and δικη 'justice', states the problem, not the solution. Why should the ways of God stand in need of any justification whatsoever? The reason, of course, is immediate if we characterize the problem by its other, more familiar title, the problem of evil. Theologically, the problem is stated precisely: how is it possible for evil to exist at all if the creator is both good and powerful? If God is good He would not want evil to exist; and if He were powerful He would be able to create a world without evil; but evil exists, and so either God does not exist or He cannot be both all-powerful and all-good.

So formulated, the problem seems to be a source of urgency only for theists; but this is to confront the problem only on the surface. Even if one does not specify God, the problem of evil persists, especially if it is wanton and random, as we have seen in the chapter on abandonment. If the world is rational, how can we make sense of undeserved suffering? If the world is irrational, how can we justify the worth of being rational ourselves? Milton's formulation of course has more impact, but it is both naive and arrogant to assume that the problem vanishes if theism is rejected. Milton and Leibniz both speak to a wider audience than their co-monotheists. If for no other reason than this, that the argument is entangled with almost all the great philosophical questions, such as freedom, evil, ignorance, justification, and reason, it deserves the attention of any thoughtful inquirer. It may be worth assuming a good and powerful God just to be able to confront such wondrous and magnificent questioning, not to mention the greatness of Milton's poetry.

For the sake of the present inquiry, however, this massive problem is relevant only in an oblique, though still powerful, way. For the argument usually develops along these lines, that some human suffering can be justified on the basis of freedom. That is, if I am morally free and hence capable of being responsible, it would seem a requisite that I am thereby enabled to do morally harmful things to others, for if I could not, then my freedom would be a sham. Thus, to allow for the obvious advantage of being free, even a good and powerful God would have to allow for my being wicked, and wickedness not only produces suffering in my victims but also allows for suffering in my punishment. This is the central focus of Milton's argument, and there seems to be some appeal in it.

But what about the suffering brought about not by human wickedness, which may be necessary for freedom, but simply by misfortune? If God must allow for the suffering brought about by human freedom, why does He allow for any other kind? Granted that the victims of Nazi and Bolshevik terror may be accounted for by the freedom of these wicked men, what about the victims of purely natural occurrences such as earthquakes, pestilence, flood, and famine? A good and powerful God should have been able to arrange such events so that they did not make the innocent suffer. Theodicists therefore distinguish between moral evil, which is the result of human responsibility and which hence can be justified on the grounds of being free, and metaphysical evil, which is unwarranted and undue suffering brought about by nonhuman agency.

But what the theodicist calls 'metaphysical evil' is precisely what interests the inquirer into fate. And so it is reasonable to attend to how the theodicists explain metaphysical evil and to what extent their reflections constitute a *justification* for unearned or undeserved suffering. The easiest way out of this dilemma is simply to deny the reality of metaphysical evil altogether by claiming either that such suffering is deserved or that it is not evil at all but mysteriously good. That is, what appears to us a misfortune is in reality good fortune. The death of an innocent child may seem horrible and unacceptable to its parents, but God in His wisdom knows that were the child to live it would fall on morally evil ways and hence lose its soul forever in hellfire and damnation. As fantastic as the account may seem, there is no doubt it does provide comfort for the religious believer. If one profoundly believes the dead child is in heaven and also believes the grief one endures is either in punishment for a past wrong or a test or strengthening of character, then such bereavement can be endured more easily, and one's sense of rationality and order is not abused.

The trouble with this account, which we can provisionally label 'naive theodicy', is that it is an amphiboly; that is, the fundamental meaning of terms is altered in the development of the argument. For the term 'good' no longer means at the end of the analysis what it means at the beginning. The argument turns on 'apparent good' and 'real good'. It may well be the case that the ravaged child goes to heaven, which is a good thing, but it cannot be said that for a child to be ravaged is a good thing. We are all quite willing to admit that many excruciating torments may have beneficial results, but this does not make the torment into a pleasure or even a good. Naive theodicy does not explain evil; it explains it away.

Neither the poet Milton nor the philosopher Leibniz is

naive, however, and neither of their respective theodicies explains evil *away*. A closer examination of Milton may show us why this is so. To be sure, the key to Milton's argument is that evil is explained by the greater worth of being free, which at first glance may seem no different than naive theodicy. God allows Adam and Eve to be tempted to disobey his command because He wants their worship of Him to be freely given rather than forced. But this violation is curious indeed, for in Eve's disobeying God the supreme father is offended. This claim stuns the mind. How could a God be offended? In particular, how could a God who values freedom be offended when this freedom is finally realized by Eve's rationalizing that possession of knowledge of good and evil is something God would want her to have? An offended God is simply not all-good and all-powerful. An offended God is a self-contradiction resulting from an overliteral anthropomorphism.

Unless, of course, by the term 'good God' one means not a God who automatically guarantees the highest degree of pleasure for His creatures but, more profoundly, a God who is good in exactly the same way that we mean a human person is good, that is, that the failures and successes of others as well as ourselves matter; and one is sympathetic to the suffering of others and is willing to forgive offenses. But this seems heretical to traditional notions of God as all-powerful. Unless, of course, one argues that only the supremely powerful are those willing to let others be free; that power is far, far more evidenced in its surrender than in its employment. God becomes therefore all-good not in the sense that He guarantees happiness for all but in the more original sense of good that allows for the *worth* of others, not the happiness of others. God is all-powerful not in the sense that He continues to run the entire universe by His energy and direction but in the way a great leader of a free nation is powerful in that he *lets be* the autonomy of the people.

Milton's argument suggests that Eve's rebellion merely

completes her creation as a free being. She did not have to
eat of the fruit from the forbidden tree; indeed she is free
(doomed) the moment she begins to *think*. For once Eve
thinks about her own ignorance of good and evil and recognizes that such ignorance makes her a less worthy worshiper
of God, she is already deprived of her essence as the woman
of paradise and is no longer innocent. The archangel need not
drive her from Eden; by her own freedom and thinking she
realizes that Eden, where one is automatically happy, simply
is not for her.

Milton's poetry therefore establishes a truly remarkable
transformation of meanings. 'Powerful', in the divine sense,
does not mean 'able to *do anything*' but rather means 'able to
allow anything'. And 'good' does not mean 'making people
happy' but rather means 'letting people forge their own
worth'. Rather than intervening in the affairs of men the way
an operator interferes in the realm of a machine, Milton's God
shares in the joys and anguish, the success and failure of his
beloved creatures. Parents often are overwhelmed by their
own realization that their love of their offspring demands they
allow their children to hazard and risk their own safety and
advantage. This is what it means for a religious figure to clepe
his God as "Father"; this is something a theologian has extreme difficulty in doing since the theologian wants to *explain*
whereas the religious figure wants to *understand*.

If one objects that an all-powerful God is required by His
own omnipotence to arrange things in the world so that no
undeserved suffering occurs, this is to equate erroneously the
notion of goodness with that of justice. But no finite being
could possibly opt for an absolutely just God bereft of any
mercy or compassion. The term 'goodness' simply cannot be
reduced to 'doing only what is just', for that, quite simply, is
not what goodness means. Is God, then, unjust? In order to
be good, He must be. This is not heresy even for traditional
Christians because God also is merciful. It merely means that

justice is a virtue and hence can be ranked in importance; it is not goodness, for goodness is what the virtues are designed to achieve. Strictly speaking, it is not required to assert that God is unjust but simply to say that God is nonjust; for justice is a virtue only when it serves goodness.

But Milton's theodicy, stunning as it is, concerns itself only with what the theologians call 'moral evil', which can be justified by the need for autonomous worth, sometimes dangerously identified as freedom. But the inquirer into fate is more interested in what the theologians call 'metaphysical evil', that is, evil that is irrelevant to human freedom and responsibility. To appreciate the theodicists' contribution to this problem we must turn to Leibniz, who was twenty-eight years old when Milton died in 1674. It is entirely remarkable that in such a brief period two thinkers, so unalike in other ways, would be so contemporary in their struggle with thinking about evil. Perhaps the time simply was ripe for theodicy; certainly no contemporary thinking on this almost forgotten question equals theirs.

Leibniz approaches this problem of undeserved evil in the same spirit that Milton approaches moral evil. God, Leibniz argues, does not intervene directly in the affairs of this world; rather He selects the best among possible worlds. After the recent achievements of the enlightened twentieth century and its Auschwitzes and Soviet gulags and its grim genocides, the claim by Leibniz that this is the best of all possible worlds seems both childish and offensive. Tell it to the victims of Stalin, Hitler, Idi Amin, and the Khmer Rouge. No one can believe that *this* is the best of all possible worlds. Perhaps it is not even a good world at all!

But these protests are, as is usual with self-indulgent modernists, entirely irrelevant. According to Leibniz, God does not choose the most just world, and certainly not the happiest. Instead He judges not on the principles of prudence or success but simply on the principle of perfection. That is, again, the choice is based not on what happens in this world but on what happens among worlds. But how can we choose among worlds we do not understand? The answer is, we cannot. So Leibniz is simply speaking nonsense. But Leibniz says not that *we* can choose among possible worlds but only that God can choose; and the basis of his choice is *not* justice in this world or happiness in this world. The choice is based on God's nature as perfect. And what makes it perfect is not that it is good or just but simply that it is bestowed to us as a gift whereby we alone can become worthy of who we are—not that we can live in it more happily than anywhere else.

Now Voltaire, of course, has huge fun poking at this theodicy; and indeed any scoffer such as Voltaire, witty, cunning, and brittle, can easily puncture this inflated bubble. Leibniz, not gifted as was his contemporary fellow theodicist, was unfortunate indeed in his choice of words. But in philosophy it is principles and argumentation that count. Among possible worlds is chosen this one world, in which random as well as deliberate evil proliferates, because in this world, and only in this world, *we* do exist and *we* do matter. And in part we matter because we are fated.

This may seem to say little more than that the real world, because it actually exists, is more perfect than a possible happier world simply because the former is real and the latter an illusion. But can *we*, as finite sufferers in this real world, actually imagine another world in which *we* exist? But who *we* are depends on *this* world and whatever we imagine is part of this world, whether we call it another world or not. For this 'imagining' stems from our own consciousness, and as long as we are doing the imagining, the object of such imagination cannot logically exclude the imaginer, which is what another 'world' would imply. Thus we may easily imagine circumstances in this world to be better, but not the world itself to be otherwise, for such another world would have to exclude *us*, and hence the word 'better' has subtly changed its meaning.

There is, to be sure, a touch of arrogance in the claim that the most perfect world would be one in which we were in a constant state of delirious rapture and joy. The claim would be especially dubious if such happiness were undeserved, which for most of us would have to be the case. What is important for those concerned with the question of fate in this analysis is that the naive theodicist approaches the problem solely from the perspective of what the term 'evil' means (is it 'evil' for us to endure undeserved suffering?), whereas the enlightened theodicists like Milton and Leibniz approach the same problem from a consideration of what the term 'good' means. And once the term 'good' is given a moral rather than prudential sense, the problem is rendered free from self-contradiction. For to be able to achieve one's own moral worth through freely deserved suffering as well as through enduring undeserved suffering is thus seen as a justification of *this* world with a *morally* good and bestowing God.

Yet as profound as Milton and Leibniz may be, they both insist on justification. But the present inquiry shows that the very *meaning* of fate is inconsistent with its being justified. And so, along with the naturalist and the stoic, the theodicist must be rejected as offering meaningful accounts of fate. This rejection in no way entails a denial of any of these three accounts with regard to other explanations; perhaps there is a good and powerful God who has prepared for us a world in which we can achieve our own worth; perhaps stoic endurance does indeed strengthen character; perhaps there is comfort in the realization that nature protects species and not individuals. But none of these justifications can account for what *fate* means, for fate can only be illuminated and not justified.

The insights of both Milton and Leibniz, however, may

indeed provide some illumination in spite of their theodicy; but to the extent to which they do so, they have left theodicy itself behind. We can learn from great poets and thinkers beyond what they themselves may recognize as their contribution. For this we can be grateful and at least recognize that, this being so, ours is at least not the worst of all possible worlds.

9

■ ■ ■

ILLUMINATION

To the abandoned, the failure of these three systemic accounts to justify the banishment from whence we belong is no solace. Indeed, frail as they are, these three accounts at least offer some hope of finding a refuge in reasoned analysis, and the inquiry has shown their attempts to be unsuccessful. We remain abandoned by ourselves and from ourselves, and this deep and painful divorce is all the more cruel for its being inexplicable. And yet the journey through these three attempts to justify our fate is not without reward. Our deeper understanding of various notions such as 'good' and 'evil' provides us with the implements to dig more deeply into fated abandonment.

It is, as we have seen, impossible to speak of justifying our fates. But this does not prohibit us from seeking illumination. To justify fate is to show that what happens in fateful phenomena such as undeserved suffering ought to have happened, or at the very least should have produced some benefit as a consequence that is equal to or greater than the loss endured by the suffering. But this cannot be done, for the adjective 'undeserved' simply means that such suffering cannot be justified. To illuminate means, however, to see things in terms of the light they throw on who we are. It is now necessary to probe into this existential realm; if we cannot justify

unwarranted suffering, at least we should be able to illuminate what it means.

In the description of abandonment it was shown that the
alienation is from a home where we belong. This sense of belonging, which is now lost, gives a peculiar poignancy to fated
abandonment: it is not merely that we have no home; it is that
we are exiled from a home where we truly do belong. As rational beings we belong in a place where being rational is the
basis for membership; but the world, *our* world, provides entirely random events over which we have no control, thus
alienating us from the realm in which control and governance
matter. This alienation is called 'abandonment' because we
are removed from what is familiar and akin by forces beyond
ourselves, and there is no redress or appeal. How are we to
explain this?

The early mythmakers in almost all cultures tell stories in
which we—the species or the members of a tradition or
race—once were favored, in some sort of Eden or Paradise,
and from which we were later expelled. These early sages
were not the inventors of this self-realization but merely
those who sought to give it shape. That is, we do not believe
in this abandonment because Moses wrote the Genesis account telling of our fall; rather Moses wrote about the fall in
order to account for this a priori realization of existential abandonment. Driven from our proper place (Eden), we long to
return, but due to forces beyond our command (Satan's temp-
tation of Eve, in which we played no role) we are kept from
it. The literal belief is not necessary for the fullness of the
impact. We are governed no longer by benign and rational
forces (God?) but by random and capricious fates. If we leave
aside the question of theology, we must ask: What does this
realization tell us about ourselves? Who are we? What does it
mean to be the victims of fate and hence be abandoned by
controlled and measured reason?

We may return to the two examples in Chapter One. The
youth selects the shortest straw in the hostage situation and

cries out, "Why me?" The loving mother is marooned by paralysis forever from her life and family and pleads, "Why me?" In the urgency to give an answer, perhaps we have not reflected long enough on their questioning. To say, "This is nature's way, so accept it," is an answer of sorts that may even help the sufferer to some extent. But the Bambi fallacy is still a fallacy. To say, "Endure it, and in enduring you show strength of character," is an answer, a stoic's answer, and it too may offer brief solace. "It is God's will" may well be the most persuasive and may even comfort enough. But all three offer solace by persuading the sufferer not to ask. By giving an answer, the asking is terminated. To continue to ask is simply to augment the suffering.

But why do these sufferers ask this question at all? They do not raise the question merely as a protest. They may, perhaps, realize nothing can be done. But they still ask. And so the focus of the inquiry must now become, what does this *asking* mean? What does this *asking* tell us about who we are?

To *ask* this question in itself already reveals. It reveals, first and foremost, that truth matters; and second, almost equal to the first, it reveals that *we* matter individually: not just nature, or God, or our moral character, but *us*. And, peculiarly, the stroke of fortune focuses not on the species or on God or on moral character but on *us*.

Why me? Because *I* matter. Why *ask* 'why me?' Because truth matters. These two revelations provided just by the *question* itself need to be considered, perhaps far more profoundly than any answer. But now it seems we are compelled to ask 'matters to whom?' Does not the notion of 'mattering' always presuppose an indirect object, an agent who cares? A child *matters* to her mother; without the mother or a surrogate, can it *mean* anything to say simply that the child just *matters*, period? But if 'to matter' requires a caring agent, then there can be no universality or authority unless this agent is identified; and even then the agent may or may not always care, which renders 'mattering' an entirely relative and subjective affair. This, however, is what the present inquiry denies. To say that 'I matter' or that 'truth matters' does not require a subjective opinion of one who cares. To show this, and at the same time to penetrate more deeply into the meaning of fate, an extended analysis or argumentation must be presented. In what follows, the analysis proceeds first by a consideration of the way we commonly make ordinary judgments in ordinary language. Only after these ordinary judgments are revealed can we then press for the deeper existential meaning that lies beneath them. We assume, then, the following situations.

■   ■   ■

1. A leopard kills an impala. This is seen as an act of nature. Although the impala's mate, parent, or offspring may manifest some grief at this, we seem to accept the grief as part of nature too. We see neither the killing nor the putative grief of the impala's kin as evil, immoral, or as demanding some special account. To this extent, the death of the impala, particularly if we focus on *this* impala, does not matter. By saying this we mean that nature in no way provides us with any device that can be used for thinking selectively about the death of this one antelope within the herd. If one were to argue that the death of *this* antelope matters or even that the impala herself matters, which would make her undeserved death stand out, one would imply that such a purely natural phenomenon is somehow unreasonable. It is simply not within the maxims and principles of nature that any individual can matter. It is not what we *mean* by nature.

2. A man murders his wife. Here the death matters *absolutely*, that is, morally, and morality is a lawlike system of rules and principles with universal significance. Here we do not need to add the subjectivist addendum 'to whom' when we say she matters and that her death matters. Even if I do not know her name or her circumstances I can say, "She ought not to have been murdered," which carries with it the presup-

position that she mattered. If she had not mattered, her death would not have upset the moral law or provoked the machinery of justice. Even if no one liked her at all and no one grieves for her, her death demands judgment. The *right* of the victim was thwarted and the *guilt* of the perpetrator is ascribed. Thus she matters.

3. A wanton teenager wanders onto the veldt and, merely for bloodsport and the satisfaction of his perverse pleasure in cruelty, kills the impala. Does the impala *now* matter? Or do we simply say that the wickedness of the youth matters? The impala when killed by the leopard does not matter; then why does the impala matter when killed by the boy? The impala does not matter even now; it is the boy who matters. He is judged as cruel and wicked.

4. A hungry leopard kills a human child who has wandered onto the veldt. This death matters. Above, in (3), it is not the death but the killing that matters. Now the death matters because the child matters. The leopard in no way is blamed; there is no moral violation at all. Still, the child matters. Why? Because the child is not merely a *what* but a *who*. His death matters absolutely, as does the death of the wife in (2), but unlike the death of the wife his death matters *not* because of the universality of the moral law. There is nothing moral or immoral about a leopard killing a human child. The child's mattering is not due exclusively to the grief of the parents and kin but is absolute. It is the boy's fate, not the wickedness of the leopard, that makes the boy and his dying *matter* absolutely. Hence it is fate that grounds the mattering of the luckless boy's death.

■   ■   ■

Would we say that the impala, in the first scenario, was fated? Not if this analysis is correct. These are the ways we think. Fate is therefore only of persons, not of entities in nature. To be fated is to be a *who*. But if the reasoning is valid, then there is no *who* in nature. But it also follows that *who* one is cannot be exhaustively accounted for by moral reasoning. Otherwise the child's death by the leopard would not matter. Thus, what it means to be a *who* rather than a *what* is not only to be morally significant but also to be able to be *fated*.

These analyses, of course, omit the more extreme protests of the advocates of animal rights who base their moral views on the metaphysical claims that human beings have no special status as morally significant beings. This omission avoids distracting the inquiry from its true purpose. It is not important that the metaphysical status of animals is judged correctly, for the argument could be characterized by an assumption: "Let us assume there are such entities as impalas whose individual deaths are not morally relevant." The appeal to ordinary language is meant to show how one thinks—or can think—about fate; and to this extent the analysis of these scenarios is beneficial.

The most important point that emerges (aside from the clarification of the notion that 'I matter' is not dependent on a subject who cares) is that only a 'who' can be fated; there is no fate for a 'what'. It was fate that the boy happened to wander out onto the veldt at the same time the hungry leopard was in the vicinity. As such, his fate illuminates who he is, and individualizes. As we have seen, nature does not individualize; guilt and deprivation of rights do individualize, but fate, which is morally neutral and irrelevant, also individualizes. It makes the *story* of the boy; but apparently it does not make a story for the impala, unless an artist employs anthropomorphism to create a character similar to Bambi.

But if an impala has no fate, we must ask why. Is it because the impala is not on a morally equal status with humans? But fate is irrelevant to morality; it rains upon the just and the unjust. Perhaps, as we have seen in the earlier sections, it is because the boy on the veldt has a story; the impala, being entirely replaceable, does not. This is surely a significant point, but it does not entirely satisfy. Why say the boy is fated at all? Is it not because the random death by the leopard is left unjustified by mere moral reasoning yet one feels there should be *some* reason? That is, is the *questioning* of fate itself not a hostage to our reason? If it seems there is no *reason* available to account for the death, then, as thinkers, we become aware of a curious lack in our understanding. The long history of fate and the belief in destiny is due, therefore, to an expectation that our reason should be able to find some account that makes sense of such wanton occurrences. But if the impala has no fate, it must be because the victim is not of a rational species. That is, we *expect* there to be a reason, of some sort, to account for undeserved suffering of reasoning beings. Thus the phenomenon of people appealing to fate is in fact an indication of their expectation that reason should be able to account for existential meaning.

And here, of course, is the crucial turning point of the argument. As reasoning beings we demand some kind of sense to be thrown on this question of how to *think* about an individual's fate. We have discovered that such reasoning cannot *justify*; it is independent of morality; it is inexplicable by natural causes or metaphysical accounts. And yet the question is still *asked*. Then we must either deny that the question itself is intelligible or forge or discover a unique realm of interrogation in which such questioning does indeed make sense. The sheer enormity of the question 'why me?' prohibits us from simply dismissing it as meaningless. That is, unless such questions are meaningful, the very limit and range of meaning are violated. But the discovered limitations of justification require that we now turn to reason not merely as a resource for ascribing responsibility or agency but as a source of illumination. That is, we realize that as reasoning beings our capacity to think with some authority must also include the realm of truth for its own sake. To "illumine" means to render capable of being thought about *as* meaningful. And if this probing is essentially sound, this in turn must mean that we can think about what it means to be fated.

Why should I be selected by capricious fate to suffer what

others do not? Suppose I were able to discover an answer that renders my selection determinable by principles, however vague. Then, indeed, the term 'I' is nothing more than the result of all these principles taken together: nature, morality, metaphysics, and the rules of fate. But there are no *rules* of fate. Just because there are no rules of fate, who I am has a uniqueness that otherwise it could not have. In the absence of fate, the sole determiner of uniqueness that can be thought about would be *moral*; that is, I am unique solely because I alone am responsible for my free acts, my guilt. But as we have seen in the chapter on chance (the gambler), a world in which reason is restricted to principles that must determine what is the case according to inexorable laws, even moral laws, permits of nothing that singles me out as mattering just because of who I am. Thus it is because I am fated that I matter: that is, because there *are* no rules that exhaustively account for all that I am and what happens to me, my existence is isolated as something that stands out over and against all determinable rules. This would be misology *only* if we restrict the term 'reason' to justificatory functions. But reason can also illuminate simply who I am, and precisely to the extent that this 'who' matters independently of justification.

It is therefore essential to our understanding of fate that we examine what it means to say "I matter." There are four distinct and important variations of what this means.

■　■　■

1. I matter because my friends and family care about me. This is the form that asks "to whom" do I matter. It relies on the care of others and hence is not absolute. If the impala's death does cause a kind of grief in its mate, then in this sense the impala also *matters*. This is not an unimportant form of mattering, but it is a contingent one. When reason appeals to this form it seeks justification.

2. I matter because of my responsible, free acts. This is

an absolute form of mattering, because the violation of the moral law evokes a universal censure, and the rules of decent behavior are not contingent but absolute. If I am guilty I should be punished, whether anyone cares for me or not; if I am a victim I deserve redress, whether anyone likes me or not. Hence this form of mattering is both absolute and justificatory.

3. I matter because of my inheritance. I am born American, male, white, left-handed, and so on. As such I inherit certain physical qualities as well as values and traditions. These matter independently of an agent who cares, so they too are absolute, not contingent. When reason appeals to this form, however, it yields no justification but only illumination.

4. I matter because of my fate. The reality of my being both favored and victimized by uncontrolled forces establishes my uniqueness in the development of my story. Unlike the case of (3) above, in which I matter solely because of what I inherit as this man's child, that woman's son, in fate I matter because my meaning is not exhausted by rule-governed disciplines such as the laws of genetics or the principles of morality. My story is unique to me, as is my guilt, but guilt is determined by universal laws whereas my story is controlled in part by capricious fates. The impala has no fate because she is understood solely as a creature in nature. She cannot ask 'why me?' because she cannot ask 'why' at all. This selection by random forces makes my unique story matter, but reason cannot justify this but only illuminate it.

■　　■　　■

These are the four ways to matter. The first two are justificatory, and the second two are illuminating of my existence. The first two make sense because of how we think about events, as either natural or moral; the second two make sense because of how we think about meanings.

But the last two ways in which I can be said to matter presuppose a suppressed premise, namely, that truth matters. Or, to be more precise, I must be understood as that kind of being for whom truth matters before I can matter in these two ways. In other words, being fated reveals the truth about my finitude, but unless this truth is of sufficient import to warrant the agony of my fated suffering, I cannot make sense of it. This truth in no way justifies my suffering, of course; but if truth matters, and if such truth is made available only through fate, then it is at least thinkable. But in order for this argument to be persuasive, one must first assume that we do not accept being deceived about who we are. We care about the truth of our existence on two levels: What does it mean to be a human being at all? This might be called the universal sense of meaning. But we also seek to understand what it means to be this particular human being. These questions interrelate; for what it *means* to be a human being at all is to care about what it means to be *this* human being. Astonishingly, what it means to be an impala completely explains this or that impala; but what it means to be a 'who' does not explain what it means to be *this* who. Because I alone must endure and enjoy the peculiarities of my fate, to be *who* I am must include a reverence for the truth of my existence.

It is astonishing indeed to discover from these analyses that the impala has no fate; but reflection upon the meanings of these terms permits of no other inference. We appeal to the notion of fate simply because what happens to us in ungoverned events is not deserved. But this presupposes two important principles: first, that I *am* free, or otherwise I could not deserve *anything*, so that the lack of desert in fate is no more remarkable than any other joy or suffering; second, that the mind appeals to fate precisely because all other forms of explanation seem lacking, and we cannot abandon reason's demand that some sense of explanation must be available for everything. Ephemeral as 'fate' is, it nevertheless stems from our rational nature. But impalas are neither free (in a moral sense) nor rational, and so they have no fate. This is itself less important than what it reveals about fate itself: that fate is not about a world of random events but about us. It also presupposes the hugely important realization that we expect our reason to supply us not only with natural accounts and moral principles but also with existential truth. For the argument is basically simple: if, in fate, I endure undeserved suffering or unearned joy, such occasions are inexplicable by appeal either to science or to morality; yet in the very *asking* of the question "why me?" we expose our expectation that reason should provide a response. The only kind of response possible is that which would illuminate what it means for us to be who we are. Thus fate is meaningful not as a metaphysical power but as an existential truth.

This discovery is indeed remarkable. But in order to carry out the implications, we must now turn to the next section in which each of the salient elements is examined in greater detail.

PART FOUR

THE

FATED

WHO

.   .   .

10
. . .

THE FATED WHO

It has now come to this: the inquiry into fate has unearthed the Socratic problem, who am I? Perhaps it is inevitable that all true philosophical inquiries must ultimately confront this launching pad against which any rocket seeking the stars must first thrust its fiery jets. Who am I? The history of this curious discipline gives us several answers: I am body and soul, will and intellect, animal and spirit, phenomena and noumena, will and representation, man and superman. So often am I divided and disjoined that I may begin to wonder how many of me there are, and which bears my name.

Perhaps, before we turn to the answers to this great question, we should reflect upon what it means to ask it at all. Why do we ask it? *Who* asks it? *A victim of amnesia* may ask it in a fearsome, dreadful request for identity. "Who am I?" means "what is my name?" To whom do I belong? It must be an entirely terrifying and unholy state not to know who one is. Is this our question? But most of us are not amnesiacs, and so we know perfectly well who we are. We have this name, this address, this family, this history: perhaps that is all we need to know.

A *child* may ask this question, seeking reassurance and an embrace from a caring parent. "Who am I?" "You are our child, your name is Chris, and we love you." It is meaningful because the child is always somewhat unsure of familial acceptance and love. An *actor* may also ask this question as the players gather for rehearsal and the roles are being given out by the director. "Who am I this time?" means "what role do I play?" This too is meaningful. And although most of us are neither amnesiacs nor children nor actors, these forms of the question are not to be entirely despised; indeed, far too many philosophers overlook these queries, as if only the most abstract and formal of inquisitions deserve their concern. But their disdain is unworthy, for all forms of this question contribute to what is being asked.

"Who am I?" may also be asked of one confronting a demanding task, which seems to transcend our powers and our rights. A *petit juror,* balancing the guilt or innocence of the accused may ask, "Who am I" to judge another? The juror's form of the question is a protest against the burden of an unsought duty that appears beyond our capacity; for we are not gods but men and, unable to see into the hearts and minds of others, we dare not judge.

And when the cat, fortune, is in distemper, are we then but mice seeking dark holes to bide the sway of this fickle, feline fury until the tempest passes? Who am I that can be *victim* to such ungoverned devastation?

The questioning itself reveals. For in asking these forms of the same question we expose something about ourselves. To ask "who am I?" presupposes that it matters. We ask because we care about who we are. We are, then, beings for whom our existence matters, and the mattering is parent to the question. We could not, would not, ask who we are unless being who we are matters. But this mattering, the father to the query, needs to be provoked before the siring can produce the child. All the forms mentioned rely on some special kind of provocation: the loss of memory, the need for comfort, an assigned script to play a role, an unwanted judgment, a derailing by misfortune of our smooth journey. These provocations initiate our asking the question in these parochial ways. Because we are truth-seeking beings by nature, we are provoked to ask it on the most concrete but universal level: Who am I *at all*? Why should there be a *me*?

But the 'who' and the 'why' have already been somewhat illuminated simply by the question. Who am I? The questioner. Why am I at all? Because truth matters. These answers, of course, are neither complete nor final. But any response that does not include them suffers from bewildered distraction. Whoever I am I must include as a part of this 'who' the asking of the question. And it is in this realization that the forms of the question asked by the amnesiac, the child, the player, the juror, and the victim of misfortune are not as parochial as they first seem, for though few are amnesiacs, the question is meaningful to us all. For we all can, and do at times, *forget* who we are.

And so we must probe more deeply into the very questioning itself. Why does the amnesiac want to know who he is? Let us suppose the amnesiac is befriended by a sympathetic and wealthy family willing to incorporate him into their home. Such a one may wonder if the discovery of his real origins would be so favorable. Would he not willingly dismiss his concern and adopt the pleasanter world, accept a made-up name, and care no longer about asking who he is? We need not poll the psychologists and sociologists to find the answer. The passion to discover one's truth would be overwhelming. Not all the comforts, advantages, and pleasures of an assumed fortune could sway us from finding out who we really are. Not to know this would be a haunting, frustrating, and distracting torment that would admit of no solace or redress. We all sense this; yet why? Why should it matter so much merely to be ignorant of one's self? Though most of us have never had to endure it, surely it is because such ignorance leaves us so incomplete. Deprived of memory is equal to being deprived of a limb or an eye: it diminishes our worth by removing what is essential for being a complete 'who'. It is not that these memories need be pleasant or even desirable; it is simply that without that link to the past our story is cut off from our origins.

The child's plaintive cry for reassurance as to who she is can also be recognized as a fundamental need not to be abandoned. Vaguely aware of her total dependence upon caring others, she realizes that without some established role or place, she is nothing. It reassures her to hear her parents fondly remind her that she is theirs, that she belongs, and that her name is Chris. For that name also matters; not just to have *a* name but to have *this* name matters. Names are a part of who we are, and although we can on occasion change them, as we do when entering a religious order or when women enter into marriage, the solemnity of the change itself reminds us of the seriousness of names. A name, like a memory, is fundamental for our self-understanding.

Juliet's protest that there is nothing in a name is often misinterpreted because it is taken out of context. Shakespeare's play assures us of exactly the opposite sentiment; for it is Romeo's name as a Montague that does exactly what the young lovers say it cannot do: it destroys them utterly. Indeed, the entire balcony scene is full of lies and deceits that we the audience accept only because of their poetic beauty but that render the unfolding of the play all the more ominous. For it is in *forgetting* their names that the young lovers wreak such dismal disaster. It is not that they love that portends disaster, but their willful forgetting of who they are. Juliet asks, "What's in a name?" and Shakespeare answers, your destiny.

And speaking of plays, the actor who asks, "Who am I?" at the first gathering of the ensemble is not merely asking for the script. For if he is a good actor he realizes that he must think as the character would think if he is to do service to the play. "This time around you are Shylock." But Shylock is not merely a role, he is a character, and how one interprets a character determines the entire play. The smallest gesture, the selected gait, the measured cadence of his delivery all tell us who Shylock is, and each worthy actor adds some deepening dimension to his possibilities. There is no single way to play the role of Shylock, yet it is, for all the variations, the same Shylock throughout. This is one of the wonders we realize in the question "who am I?" There are many answers, but only one is answered. We realize that it is possible to fail at playing Shylock, so it is false to say that one interpretation is as valid as any other, for there are bad interpretations that do not fit the play. But within that one Shylock that Shakespeare bestows to us, there is no definitive, final achievement. Thus the actor's question, "Who am I?" reveals that though there is only one 'who', the faces of this *who* have, within certain limits, varied meanings. I am one, yet this one is revealed diversely. This insight will serve us in a deeper aspect as the inquiry develops.

The juror asks, "Who am I to judge this defendant?" Here the question of 'who' sounds the more ominous tone of moral isolation. We are confronted with an obligation we cannot escape yet feel ill-equipped to perform. A reasoned judgment must be made in the absence of certainty, and we cannot escape the dire responsibility of a possibly terrible consequence. From this we learn that, even with moral principles that are absolute, our ignorance offers us no excuse. If we err in our judgment we cannot seek refuge by pleading our ignorance, for the judgment remains ours forever. It is, to be sure, not completely fair; but we accept the unfairness as inevitable. Who am I to judge? The answer is that I must judge, and that very necessity, cruel in its burden, is part of how I must understand myself. Morality is not fair, it is only right; duty outranks justice. To be able to realize this truth is as awesome as any realization to which men are vulnerable.

There is a principle in ethics, often identified as Kantian, that "ought implies can," which is to say that one cannot be obliged to do what is impossible. Yet this principle is not an escapist caveat that dismisses the anguish. For I cannot *know* for certain whether this defendant is guilty or not, thereby making a guarantee of justice impossible. But this in no way absolves me from having to decide and, indeed, from bearing the burden of unsurety as long as I live. Thus 'ought' does not always imply 'can'; for as ignorant I cannot decide with the assurance that the tribunal and defendant deserve, yet I still must judge. Who am I, then, that this enormity is placed upon me? I am who I am, and being on this panel is part of who I am; and this suffices. Perfect moral laws do not make for perfect moral judgments because the judges are less than the law. The juror is moved to ask the question "who am I?" precisely because he is aware of the paradox. Yet we realize that without this dubiety there would be no moral sense whatsoever. We are thus rightly obliged to do that which is beyond our power to do rightly.

Frustrated with an important project derailed by the tiniest of the beetle's legs, we wonder who we are to be so beguiled by misfortune. Here the question is not that of the title study, "why me?" but rather "who am I to be so victimized?" It is raised partly in frustration, but also partly by expectation. Our reason seems so prolific in success, our acceptance of responsibility and the ensuing rewards or punishments seem so radiant in their clarity, that when "the cat misfortune is in distemper" we seem suddenly disarmed, as if we are ambushed by unsuspecting enemies in our own backyard. To think of fortune as a cat in distemper is to view these maverick assaults as alien but pestiferous attacks upon our proper roles. Should such a lofty being as I, capable of so much high achievement, be brought so low by trifles so insignificant they cannot even be named? Of course, we are not only confident beings but also reflective ones, and these events do make us pause. Who am I that perhaps needs reminding of my utmost frailty? One who forgets? One who, in the distraction of success, overlooks the dark cancer of fortuity that forever lurks within us? And so this form of the question particularly is important because it is a provocation of remembrance. It is as if these gremlins spaniel our heels lest we forget entirely; and this forgetting is a sabotage of truth. What is important in this last form of the question is that not only *are* we victims of wanton forces, we also forget that we are. Indeed, like the amnesiac, to forget who we are seems to be a part of who we are. We are, in our essence, self-forgetting.

The question "who am I?" is thus not an abstractionist probing; it is asked concretely by different types, such as the amnesiac, the child fearing dislocation, the actor playing a role, the petit juror, and the victims of misfortune. We must study these concrete questioners lest the urgency and meaning of the question be lost entirely. Since this point is of extreme importance, it must be pressed to show a certain weakness in philosophical methodology. An abstractionist may raise the "question of self-knowledge," which is already a step down the obscurist's path, for 'knowledge' is of objects, and the dominant persuasion of epistemologists and scientists is classification. And so what is asked fundamentally and concretely with the form "who am I?" is distorted by the artful reinterpretation of the question as one of self-knowledge. The next step along this path of misdirection is that of formalist abstraction: 'the agent' replaces the honest 'I' and 'the class' replaces the honest 'who'. "Who am I?" asks the juror; and the abstractionist responds, "An agent seeking the classificatory procedure to determine responsibility." Responsibility requires a will, and so the 'I' is classified as a will and as a knowing subject. Whether the 'knowing subject' is the same as the 'responsible will' of course then becomes a difficulty that can be sorted out only by refuge in technojargon so arcane that only experts can grapple with it. But the point is simple: it is not a disembodied 'will' that must judge and act, nor a responsible agent, but *this* particular juror who has a name, a family, and a history. 'Responsible agency' has no history, no fortune, no particularity. 'The Will'—whatever that is—does not lose sleep or have headaches, nor does it agonize over its own dubiety. It is a word given to what real jurors with real decisions actually *do*—they *will*—and in this subtle shift from the verb to the noun (they *will* because they *have* a will) the entire meaning of guilt and duty is lost forever. For we do not ask, "What is a knowing, willing agent?"—we ask, "*Who am I?*" And in order to make sense of this asking we must consider *who* does the asking. Overlooking this primary concern is a gross philosophical error, that of reifying abstractions and losing sight of the concrete reality. To ask "who am I?" without considering who asks the questions and what that question means produces ephemeral and ultimately meaningless answers. It is absurd to probe by philosophical analysis the question "who am I?" and focus solely on the kind of thing the 'agent' is without considering what the term 'who' means. Socrates was never so beguiled as this.

Each of these concrete questioners of the fundamental asking "who am I?"—from the amnesiac down through the other four—reveals a tension that exists between the two pronouns 'who' and 'I'. The amnesiac is aware of the 'I' but not of the 'who'; the actor is aware of the 'who' but not of the 'I'. The child knows it matters that the 'I' fits comfortably with the 'who'; the juror knows who he is but dreads what this 'who' will do to the 'I'; and the victim of misfortune knows the 'I' but is disturbed by the 'who'. And so in the very raising of the question, and in spotting who *asks* the question, we confront the most serious of all philosophical problems without having to abandon the concrete, familiar, and recognizable figure of the questioner himself. The question "who am I?" reveals the universal tension between the two pronouns; for the question becomes a true question only when the 'I' and the 'who' strain against each other and provoke wonder.

The 'who' is the given; the 'I' acts. *I* am free; *who* I am has a history. And so we may now pose the problem in terms of the traditional nomeclature. How can I be free if I am a 'who', that is, if I am fated?

To be fated is not to be determined, nor does it mean to assert fatalism. Rather, to be fated must be understood in the broader context of being who we are as both perpetrators and victims, players and pawns. We are, of course, determined insofar as we are natural objects; we are free insofar as we are morally responsible, and we are fated insofar as being who we are is both earned and bestowed, guided and wanton. What we must seek to do is to understand exactly how these differing ways of existing coalesce into a coherent image that can be rendered intelligible. To achieve this level of understanding we must penetrate into the mystery of 'who', which is more than merely to define the term 'who'. It is to be guided by reason, but only insofar as reason can illuminate the meanings of these various ways of existing, not by understanding reason as a determiner in a decision procedure or as a final tribunal of justification.

This inquiry into 'who' we are can be neither reductionistic nor entirely speculative. We are, first and foremost, both free and fated; and this bifurcation cannot be rendered accountable by appeals to different kinds of entities (such as 'bodies and souls') or even different realms of thinking (such as 'phenomena and noumena'). If I am free, I am free as a fated being, and if I am fated, I am fated as a free being. This is to demand that the very philosophical and fundamental meanings of these two terms require each other; or, to be dangerously blunt: I can be free only if I am fated, and I can be fated only if I am free.

In Chapter Nine we saw the first hint of how this might be possible. For if 'who' I am is rendered entirely accountable and intelligible solely by reference to rules and to principles that determine who and what I am, then any unique meaning to 'who' falls out, and I am left merely with *what* I am. So the 'who' disappears if reason is seen merely as justificatory. For 'who' under this assumption would mean nothing more than the consequences and inferential results of these various principles, whether moral, metaphysical, or natural. But such a meaning is no different than a 'what' and is entirely replaceable. Like the impala, one is just as good as another, and this is to forfeit entirely the uniqueness that comes with the term 'who'.

There is, then, as an earlier paragraph suggests, a 'mystery' of who we are. But in philosophy, 'mystery' does not mean entirely irrational or unthinkable; rather it means that which reveals itself without forfeiting its autonomy and uniqueness. I shall never be able to reduce a 'who' to a 'what', and this is due in part to the fact that a 'what' is replaceable whereas a 'who' is not. But this in no way renders a 'who' somehow irrational, though it may render it unjustifiable.

The starting point, as we suggest above, is that being fated and being free are interrelated concepts. This must now be questioned more deeply.

Can I be free *unless* I am fated? This is merely another way of asking, "can I be an 'I' unless I am a 'who'?" This seems a paradox, if not a contradiction, because to be fated is beyond my control but to be free is to assume control. Yet when *I* freely act, *who* I am is inherited and bestowed. Guilty of my wrongs, the censure is placed on *who* I am. Being born of these parents and in this culture determines *who* I am, and only because of my uniqueness can it matter who I am; but only if it matters who I am can I be free. A 'rational agent' or a 'will' is not distinct, not unique, hence cannot matter, and, not mattering, cannot be free. Conversely, it is only because I am guilty of my wrongs, and hence free, that it matters *who* I am; that is, I am determined by these parents and this culture.

But the terms 'who' and 'I' do not refer to different and distinct entities; they are two different kinds of pronouns that refer to me in different ways. Although grammarians insist that pronouns literally take the place of nouns, thereby ranking nouns as more fundamental than pronouns, philosophers reverse the hierarchy, ranking pronouns before nouns. (Descartes in the *Second Meditation* argues, "I think, therefore I am"; he does not say, "Descartes thinks, therefore Descartes exists.") So, although both 'I' and 'who' refer to one person, me, they are actually *prior* to me as an entity because their meanings, subtly though powerfully different, reveal what it means to be me.

But if there is no 'I' without a 'who' and no 'who' without an 'I', and if the latter freely acts and the former is bestowed and determined, then their mutual reference to the one person is neither contradictory nor unthinkable. To be free presupposes fortune, and being fortuned presupposes being free. Yet being free and being fortuned do not mean the same thing. Therefore we are coalescences of different meanings, represented by fundamental pronouns. And because pronouns have been shown to be philosophically prior to nouns, it is impossible to understand them in terms of their reference. Again, "I think, therefore I am" does not become meaningful or valid only after I designate the reference of the pronouns as René Descartes. So pronouns have prenominal, autonomous meanings, and the *difference* of their meanings establishes the understanding of how fate and freedom are interdependently meaningful. To be free is thus *necessarily* to be fated and to be fated *necessarily* is to be free. Because of this necessity, these pronominal meanings are a priori.

The consequences of this analysis are remarkable. For it is now impossible to think of fate as some external event that intrudes into an otherwise governed and controlled existence. Rather, the very *meaning* of my existence is both characterized and illuminated by my being fated. Obviously the specific events that affect me are not predetermined in my destiny as predictable occurrences, for that would be fatalism.

Rather, my *ability* to be victimized by random events is a *necessary* condition of who I am, and the indeterminacy of which events do indeed affect me is essential to my being meaningful *as* who I am. This is why in tragedy we can speak of inevitability without suggesting predictability. What is fundamental is *that I be vulnerable to ungoverned influences*; that is, that I am fated but not determined.

Thus fate is not external but internal to my meaning, and the truth of this is discoverable in the proper understanding of what it means to be free. In no way does this lessen any responsibility or guilt, for to be responsible I must first be a fated 'who'. This makes fate and freedom equal but opposing forces in the intelligibility of my existence. To try to render my being free as thinkable without including my being fated is simply impossible; for without fate I cannot be a 'who', and unless I am a 'who' I cannot be free. For *who* would be responsible? There must *be* a who in order for there to be ascription of responsibility, but *who* one is is bestowed by fortune.

This use of pronouns as a priori fundamental resources for an analysis of meanings is more fully developed in my book *Spirit and Existence*; and the range of its application far exceeds that of fate. There are many other dimensions of the 'who' that deserve further exploration; but such sallies go beyond the limits of the present inquiry. What belongs within this inquiry, however, is a consideration, though cursory, of what it means to recognize that our essential meaning is characterized by fate. In *Spirit and Existence* it is pointed out that our lack of pervasive control over what happens to us opens up what might be called *adventure*. That is, precisely because I do not determine everything by my own will or controls gives a certain openness to my story that can intrigue and interest me simply because it is unknown yet still a part of me. Thus by 'adventure' is meant that the world has more to offer me than I have to offer the world.

In the chapter on the gambler it was shown that a world totally governed and controlled would be bereft of play. We are playful beings just because the world offers more than we offer the world. Adventure, which both hazards and delights, is possible only if we understand by the word that which offers the unpredictable. Normally, traditional philosophers render an account of unpredictable adventure solely by an appeal to ignorance; that is, it is merely a contingent fact that we are not intelligent or erudite enough to have plotted all the molecular, subatomic, and genetic variations to the point of predictability. This means that theoretically, at least, it should be possible in some futuristic golden age to know everything about the world, thereby removing the possibility of misfortunes as well as bonanzas of good fortune. In such a golden age of predictability, knowledge would be so extensive and complete that we would have no fate at all.

But the analyses in these present chapters reveal that fate is to be understood not as the mere ignorance of the determining laws and observable factors but as an existential, a priori modality of who we are. This is due not to the limits of our knowledge but to the unlimited range of meaning. We are playful and adventuring beings; and, indeed, if the scientific advance to absolute predictability were attainable, we would still be free enough to develop even more ingenious ways of accomplishing randomness. For *who* we are can never be exhausted by nature, morality, or even metaphysics, because, as we have shown, on the existential level freedom itself requires fate.

Given my origins and my duties (the *who* and the *I*), I have a destiny; that is, I am a fated who. Sometimes, however, this coalescence of origin and duty results in a rather outstanding and impressive figure who strides through the pages of history like some knight of grand purpose whose destiny is like an armor shielding him from normal failures. The plots of most nineteenth-century operas blossom with protestations and assurances of one's destiny, as if their fortunes were as palpable as their melodies. At times these operatic heroes speak—or sing—as if destiny were an assigned and inevitable pattern of glory, bestowed by divine providence on those with enough passion to make it unavoidable. To our more cynical, realistic ears these extravagant struttings of romantic pomposity may sound childish and even ridiculous, accepted only because they are the unworthy carriages of such glorious music.

And yet is it either realistic or even critical to deny what seems so obvious? There are indeed people who seem curiously selected, almost from birth, to achieve greatness or to play a dominant role in the unfolding of high but fell events. There are a few who, spotted in their childhood as elect, pierce through the folds of their allotted time like arrows, consistently evoking from all who encounter them an aura of destiny. Surely it is not skeptical realism to deny there are such people; to be cynical does not mean to be blind. How do we account for this? To appeal to sheer accident or chance seems inconsistent with the evidence. We are willing to leave it to sheer odds when one wins the lottery or is chosen at random by the famous movie star to share the limelight on an on-spot interview. But when the forces of chance repeatedly select a single individual over and over, and when the talents, character, looks, and personality conjoin with repeated and unlikely turns and twists of fortune, it is difficult to dismiss entirely the notion that some of us are simply favored; that there is a guiding force to some that makes them the Churchills, Napoleons, Lincolns, Hitlers, Kants, Shakespeares, Attilas, and Caesars. Because coincidence is no more illuminating than destiny when stretched beyond acceptable reach, why is appeal to the former any more acceptable than to the latter? Neither is defensible by the canons of principled explanation. The appeal to destiny simply makes a better story; the appeal to coincidence simply makes for easier reliance on a mechanistic universe. But neither is intrinsically more explanatory.

Is it not possible that there is some cosmic, metaphysical force that, on occasion and in times of great urgency, selects certain already outstanding individuals for guidance and support in the achievement of dominant roles? After all, the above discussions of *who* and *I* emphasize the inherited factors that determine my physical and cultural background. But what about the chance events that happen throughout one's life and that in some cases seem to manifest such an obvious and palpable purpose that it seems sheer stubbornness to deny it? To place such momentous figures and events solely on the slender shoulders of coincidence is merely to confess one's impotence.

Such a metaphysical account is indeed possible, because it contains no self-contradictory assertions. It is also possible that there is nothing else but a purely mechanistic universe that contains odd and unexplained events merely because of the sheer vastness of interrelating causes; or it is even possible that there are completely random forces in nature. All metaphysical accounts are equally possible, and all such accounts can explain everything that happens. One cosmological system is quite literally just as good as any other in explaining absolutely everything. One can write the formula for the second law of thermodynamics on a blackboard, add to it Einstein's theory of relativity for good measure, point to these impressive formulas, and say, "That is the way water works," and thus verify Thales's cosmology. One could just as well say, "No, this is the way *air* works," and thus justify Anaximines. Neither can be falsified, and both are sufficiently elastic in their meanings that they can cover everything that happens. And so it is possible that sheer mechanism governs the universe, or that a divine mechanism governs it, or that an occasionally intrusive force enters into our otherwise naturally governed universe and guides a few remarkable people into significant and powerful destinies. But these merely show that cosmological systems in speculative metaphysics are meaningless. Nor does it help to ask which is more *likely,* since the destiny of the great is intrinsically *unlikely* in *any* system.

But if all cosmological systems are possible, and all are equal in their explanatory power, then are we left with personal preference? May one of us believe in fate as a cosmic force, another as sheer coincidence in a mechanistic universe? Such *beliefs*, grounded as they are on equally possible cosmologies, would also be equally acceptable. But even though this seems sociologically accurate, it is not philosophically worthy at all, for relativism and subjectivism are simply inimical to *truth*.

And so our problem can be simply stated. The *fact* is that there are a few rather special people who seem both favored by fortune and guided by destiny to achieve greatness. To *explain* this phenomenon seems beyond the powers of non-subjective disciplines such as metaphysics and morality, but leaving the question to subjectivist institutions such as religions or cultural systems is unworthy of philosophical thought. And, finally, the question persists even after the first points are rendered clear. What, then, are we to do?

When one writes a history of a great personage, appeal is often made to fortune or misfortune as an element in the unfolding destiny of the great figure. If Milton were not blinded in his service of the ill-fated revolution, would he have written *Paradise Lost*? In the epic the poet himself thanks God for the gift of blindness that allowed him to see more deeply into the human soul. After the event, of course, it is possible to see a connection; and because the consequence of this connection is so remarkable, we seem to think of the development as inevitable. But this only occurs *after* the events, and so it takes on the qualities of an interpretation. But is this really so unusual? It is only after the apple falls that we speculate on the nature of gravity. As we have seen in the chapter on the historian, there is a legitimate *narrative* inevitability, which depends upon the telling of the story but nevertheless illuminates with authority greater than mere interpretation, because not all stories are equally successful in providing this narrative cohesion.

This story-provided cohesion of narrative-destiny is neither relativistic nor subjectivistic merely because it comes after the events and relies on a teller. For, as we have seen, the *telling* of a story can reveal *truth*; and by this we mean not the mere accurate correspondence of the events described with the events as they occurred; rather we mean that the *story* itself can be true, that is, the connecting thematic line or plot that makes sense of discrete events. But because such *tellings* can be true, we are not restricted to purely subjectivist interpretations when we unfold the inevitability of a great man's destiny.

What is the metaphysical *cause* of this narrative inevitability that reveals the destiny of the figure's story? We cannot discern this with the cognitive powers of mere mortal beings. Besides, if we *were* able to give a *causal* account, it would then no longer be narrative inevitability but scientific predictability. What, then, does "inevitability" mean in this special sense? It is a term that applies solely to stories, not chronicles or mere recountings of events. In the climax of the story one can see the origins that make it coherent *as* a story, so that the *meaning* of the development from beginning, through the middle, and to the end, is seen as coherent just because the beginning in light of the final climax shows that the climax 'follows' from the first chapters. Here, 'follows' is neither causal nor formal but is yet authoritative; it is to say, now that the story is told I can see that, given the hero's character and these ungoverned events, the conclusion follows in a way that can be *thought* and not merely *discovered.* To *think* is to appreciate connections in terms of authority, such as rules or principles or, in this case, narrative necessity— inevitability. Thus, in Puccini's final opera, when Calif protests in the first act that it is his *destiny* to conquer Turandot or when he sings that he is *fated* to woo the icy princess, what he says can be interpreted philosophically in the following manner: "When my story is told it will be seen that the present state of my existence is linked to my ultimate success as inevitable, though not as determined." This means that the various phases of our temporal existence can be *thought* rather than merely *experienced*. We are beings in time, and if the journey itself through our history were intelligible solely by reference to the stages along the way, this would deny thinkability to my existence as such and reserve it only for the places and moments along the way. But it is my process from birth through life to death that is ultimately who I am. And so it develops that inevitability is what makes our temporal existence unfolding as a story thinkable. To unfold the meaning of existence is truth; hence to tell a story is to unfold truth. This point will be further developed in the final chapter.

One final consideration must be made on this fecund little question "who am I?" We note the two pronouns 'who' and 'I' surround a verb. Often the verb 'to be' is seen merely as a linkage (a 'copulate') between two other terms, as in class membership or identity. But the first person singular, 'am', suggests not merely the connection between the two pronouns but also a form of being. Thus the pronoun of agency (the 'I') is not only *linked* to the pronoun of inheritance (the 'who') but is also enclosed by these two pronouns as a way of existing. The 'I' and the 'who' enclose existence. This suggests that what conjoins and separates the two pronouns is the meaning of existence as expressed in the only form that necessarily designates the first person. "Who *am* I?" therefore asks not only about the 'who' and the 'I' but also about the *am*: it is a question about the meaning of existence. When this question is raised by the victim of fate, the 'am' takes on a special significance as well; namely, what is the meaning of my story? So the 'am' becomes 'unfolding'; and the question is, "who unfolds the meaning of the I?" The tense of the verb establishes the question in medias res: who am I in the midst of this unfolding story? The question underscores the existential inquiry, for *who* is always in *time*. The pronouns enclose the verb and give it meaning. But if this is true, what it means to be at all can be raised only in terms of these wedded pronouns: to understand the meaning of our existence is to understand that we are both bestowed and capable of agency. Thus each of the three terms that make up this fundamental question reveals philosophical richness. The title question "why me?" is given a meaningful response in the analysis of what makes it possible to ask "who am I?" We ask, "Why me?" and we hear the answer, "Because of who I am."

CHAPTER

11

. . .

DEATH

There is nothing of which we are more certain, yet about which we have so little comprehension, as our impending death. In no instance is the assertion that necessity brings understanding rendered so ludicrous. That we are all going to die is a fact all mature people know, yet what it means is one of our greatest mysteries. It is perhaps more insightful, however, to say that all of us are *fated* to die; for the addition of that single term becomes pivotal in our philosophical inquiry.

Yet this apparently known fact may itself be questionable. Certainly there are many who believe in an afterlife, in which one's personal identity continues in some other form, which would seem to imply that *they* really do not believe in death except perhaps as a mere transition to another state. To those for whom death means the cessation of personal existence, then, it would be improper to say that we all know we are going to die, since if it is *known* by all, the meaning would have to be the same. And because there is manifestly considerable disagreement about what it means, to claim necessity concerning its advent may be premature. Perhaps it is sufficient to admit that, in the final analysis, we really do not know what death is at all.

Epicurus, in his attempt to persuade his followers that death is not to be feared, has left us a most frustrating argument. You will never meet death, he argues, for if death is there, you are not; if you are there, death is not; hence you will never meet death. The trouble with this argument is that it is so compelling it also puts death out of our epistemic reach. We will never know what death is, for to know anything we must still be alive, and if we are alive we cannot know death directly; and if we are dead we know nothing at all.

We surely know others have died; but the death of others cannot provide us with what we most want to know. It is simply beyond our powers to know what it is like to be dead, if for no other reason than that surely death is un*like* any other state; and if death truly is the cessation of all conscious existence, then it is impossible to know what it means to die.

Yet what is stated in the opening paragraph is still true enough. Our mortality is inevitable, whatever it means. To say we are *fated* to die, however, is far more revealing philosophically; for in this realization we avoid the Epicurean paradox by focusing not on the dying itself but simply on what our mortality means to us, the living. And the most immediate and obvious truth that confronts us when we shift the focus of the question is that in the realization that we are *fated* to die, we learn a great deal about fate. For here is something that is obviously inevitable; it looms before us as a terminus; it completes the narrative structure of beginning, middle, and end; and it is, above all, undeserved. For death is neither the punitive consequence of any moral failure nor the long-desired reward of a deserving laborer. We can make no sense of it *except* as inevitable and bestowed. That these reflections entail that birth also is undeserved and bestowed, though perhaps not inevitable, is also richly deserving of our reflection. For we are, after all, seeking in this inquiry to understand what it means to be fated, and in the confrontation of an inevitable death we are guaranteed of its reality. Perhaps if we can grasp what it means to be fated to die, we can glean insight into what it means to be fated at all.

To say we are fated to die does not merely assert that we

will die, or even that we must die. Rather it says that for us
to be at all is understandable only as a transition from a beginning to an end, in which the passage itself is meaningful. That
our death is inevitable renders intelligible our existence; it is
to say that *who* we are unfolds as a destined narrative, the
very unfolding of which is truth. The end of life is not a mere
cessation; it is the terminus that, together with the opposing
terminus of birth, makes the story coherent. If this is true,
however, then the narrative sequence is the ultimate presupposition of meaning. What we commonly call 'life' is therefore
not a state or a quality but a fundamental presupposition for
meaningful events, decisions, and occurrences, some of
which are governed by our own will and some of which are
given or bestowed by forces beyond ourselves. Life therefore
is not merely what *happens* to us but also what makes who we
are possible at all. To think of ourselves as fated to die is
therefore to characterize our essential existence as 'tellable';
that is, our story can be told. As long as we are in the midst
of this sequence, we are necessarily unfinished or incomplete. To the extent to which this tale is controlled by our own
initiative we are agents within the unfolding narrative; but to
the extent to which the tale is woven by forces beyond our
control we are bestowed characters that constitute who we
are. We both make things happen and are made to endure
things happening to us.

There are those who, reflecting on the fleeting brevity of
this allotted time, emphasize the element of agency. They
urge us to make of every moment and every opportunity the
fullest use. *Carpe diem!* Squeeze from every given moment
the maximum advantage, pleasure, and profit; for otherwise
the passing hours are wasted. The notion suggests that an
hour wasted is an hour lost, as if to remain inactive is tanta-
mount to shortening one's life. The very idea that one can
waste time implies that time is to be *used* and that one is
foolish or even wicked to allow an unused hour to slip by idly

or unnoticed. Time is seen as a kind of exchequer, and thrift of these temporal shekels is the supreme virtue.

In contrast to the view of *carpe diem* is the opposing image in which one savors what is bestowed; this view is often characterized by the phrase *amor fati*. If one is so busy *using* time, it is argued, one will not allow time to bestow anything on *us*. If I seize every moment I forfeit the ability of the moment to seize me. The first urges us, "Don't just sit there, *do* something!" The second urges us, "Don't just *do* something, sit there!" Of course, the views expressed both by *carpe diem* and by *amor fati* are extremist positions, although the former is probably more misleading than the latter, since it suggests the greater illusion that in the final analysis it is what we *do* rather than who we *are* that determines a worthy story. The former, indeed, emphasizes *life*, the latter *existence*; and life is the enemy of existence.

But these appeals to what amounts to common adages are made not for their own sakes but to show that how we confront death determines how we confront life. And although the vulgar wisdom of adages may not be philosophy, they often reflect what are indeed deeper insights worthy of our concern. Does the truth of our being fated to die in any way tell us how to live? Certainly not in and of itself, for there is truth in both *carpe diem* and *amor fati*. Yet any approach that somehow denies or distracts us from the truth of this fate should be avoided if only because truth matters, and this again persuades us to reject the simplistic appeal of *carpe diem*.

Those who espouse one or the other of these two common views probably do so more on the basis of their personality than their thought; and within limits this is most likely proper. Nevertheless, the difference between these death-confronting attitudes, vulgar and simplistic though they may be, is philosophically significant. For it suggests not merely a difference of *attitude* toward life but a difference of *thought* toward fate. Granted that we are fated to die, what does this reveal about how we should think about fate altogether? The advocates of *carpe diem* seek their answer in distraction, those of *amor fati* in benumbed fascination; and therefore neither is worthy of serious reflection. But we need not yield to such exaggerated instances, nor can we dismiss entirely the reasoning behind these overstated and simplistic views. There is a serious question here. Is it more meaningful to resist the influences of fate and seek to control as much as possible? Or is there wisdom in accepting fate, and in the acceptance to learn the meaning of who we are?

This question confronts the wisdom of Aristotle with the wisdom of Job. It must be stressed that this juxtaposition of Aristotle and Job is about their wisdom and not their attitude: when confronting such profound thinkers it is always their approach to truth and not their approach to action that matters. Aristotle argues in the *Nichomachean Ethics* that of the three possible lives—pleasure, honor, and thought—the first two are deficient precisely because they rely on factors outside oneself. Only the life of thought is immune from such dependence, and hence it should be ranked as best among the three. The presupposition behind this argument is what matters here, for the argument itself is valid only if it is better to be in control. Job, on the other hand, argues the following way: if I am blessed by good fortune it is worthy simply because it is bestowed, not because it is earned. When these bestowals are unfortunate, however, lesser thinkers may assume that they must be cursed, for if good fortune is praised it makes sense that bad fortune should be cursed. But Job argues that, although we *prefer* good fortune over bad fortune—otherwise Job would be perverse—we cannot curse being fated at all. If I do not deserve my good fortune, neither do I deserve my bad; but since neither good nor bad fortune concerns deserts, I have no moral complaint about the bad.

For if it is *unjust* to have misfortune it would be *just* to have good fortune, which is ridiculous. Thus wisdom consists in the recognition that bestowals reflect our unearned worth, and therefore being able to receive bestowals *at all*, whether good or bad, illumines our truth as created beings.

Put this way, the wisdom of Aristotle, which emphasizes the existential worth of the *I*, and the wisdom of Job, which emphasizes the worth of the *who*, seem conflicting in the question "who am I?" But this conflict also mirrors a shared truth. For both thinkers ultimately recognize that what anchors the worth of their existence is truth, Aristotle in searching for it, Job in accepting it. In the biblical story, Job is already designated as a morally good man; Aristotle also argues that being virtuous (or good) is the whole point in assessing wisdom to be a virtue. Thus their respective arguments are not that it is *morally* better either to control or to be controlled but that it is *wiser* to be one or the other; and since wisdom, not to be confused with prudence, is the virtue in which truth matters, we can see that the dispute is about truth. Is truth served by seeking maximum control or is it served by letting truth control us?

However we answer this question, it should be obvious that our very understanding of truth is influenced by our being fated to die. For the existential certainty of our mortality and finitude, coupled with innate bewilderment of what death means, reveals that as beings for whom truth matters we expect from truth not the blinding clarity of a divine intuition but the ever-revealing, ever-concealing unfolding of narrative, fated, meaning. For we may scorn the nineteenth-century romantic who bravely sings of his destiny to win the icy Turandot, because we know that too often our projects are derailed by the very fateful wantonness to which he appeals in his assurance. But we can sing or wail that our destiny is ultimately death and know that this is true. It is true not as a

predictable fact in the future but as an inevitable consequence of our meaning. This is who we call ourselves, mortals, and it is only as mortals that our existence makes sense
and even truth makes sense.

Yet fully aware of our inevitable mortality, we struggle
against this fate as if it were our fate to do so. This struggle is
not merely that which we share with the animals in the instinct to preserve and to sustain our individual lives; the
struggle is to overreach the inevitable by participation in eternality through the noblest endeavors available to us, such as
art, culture, religion, and history. Though we are not eternal,
our fate seems to be to have eternity matter, and not in the
mere faith of some post-terrestrial existence but in how we
guide our reluctant destinies. As fated to die, we are acutely
conscious of the eternal as a beckoning, even as a home beckons an exile. And so in our finest moments we assign the quality of eternality to those monuments that most reveal the
truth of this fated struggle against fate. We speak of the "immortal Shakespeare" not because his works outlasted his life
but because in these works we find jeweled reflectors of everlasting meaning.

And this is why so much is gained by the insertion of fate
into our claims about death. We say that we are *fated* to die
and not that we are *going* to die because we are not merely
mortal but mortals imposed like decals on the pane through
which eternal light streams as an alluring beacon, or perhaps
like finite silhouettes darkly shadowed against the infinite
sun. To speak of our own mortality as our destiny is to achieve
a kind of mastery over our fate; for the *recognition* of the fateful in our mortality reveals the truth in our narrative destinies, a truth that is universal, eternal, and immortal.

In the same way that our freedom is meaningful only if we
are fated, so our mortality is meaningful only because of the
truth of the eternal and the eternality of the true. It is as
bootless to resist death by the idolatry of health regimes or

the refuge of cowardice as to deny the eternal by the frantic distractions of *carpe diem*. We may be mortals, but we are not bereft of infinite susceptibility to everlasting truth. It is our fate to die; but it is also our fate to overreach death by our art and our worship.

We may be asked the speculative, metaphysical question, "Do we have immortal souls?" An honest confession of ignorance may be our only acceptable reply to this question. But to respond in another way, by claiming, "It is our fate to die," we both affirm and deny what is asked; for it is undeniably true that it is our fate that eternality matters and that the eternal resides in our greatest achievements of art and religion. It is just as undeniable that our fate is to be confounded in metaphysics—that is, not to *know* the answer to the question—and that our fate is to die. This may not comfort the terminally ill—a class to which we all belong in varying degrees of urgency—or one grieving for the death of a beloved, but this is due to the very finitude of our reasoning and understanding. In this question we cannot justify, but we can illuminate. In this inquiry we do not seek justification; we seek illumination.

That we are fated to die, then, tells us less about death than about fate; but being death-fated is so fundamental a part of us that this development is not without influence on our understanding of mortality. Death, as Hamlet tell us, is "that undiscovered country from whose bourne no traveler returns" (III, 1) and hence must always be somewhat mysterious, though inevitable. Being fated to die, however, is discoverable, for it is how we are. What does it tell us?

It is as if we were created. For if we are created, our story cannot only be *tellable*, it can indeed be told and heard. As creatures our stories have an audience; as creatures we do not create the roles, but we can interpret them. It is as if there is a teller of the tales, the plots of which, being in the midst of them, we cannot see, but as the lines unfold, the role we play is revealed. Such a creator, however, would have to be of the Miltonian kind: a dramatist whose creations are meant to develop from what is bestowed to a bestowing agent, a creature who through his self-developing freedom completes the creative act yet remains bereft of certain knowledge about the ultimate questions. In other words, for us to be fated to die makes existential and narrative sense only because the unfolding of our destiny reveals who we are as if we were created. Our existence itself begins as a bestowal and unfolds our autonomy, giving an *I* to the given *who,* whose belonging in a dramatic plot is inevitable. To be fated to die reveals this belonging. Merely to die leaves us without such belonging: we must be *fated* to die in order for this belonging to be achieved.

Does this imply that such reasoning depends on an option of belief? That if one believes in a bestowing creator, then one can think we are fated to die; whereas if one does not believe in a bestowing creator, then one must be content with merely realizing we shall die? Not at all. Rather, the existential reasoning precedes whatever metaphysical beliefs one may have. Because any metaphysical certainty is denied us, such assertions or denials would be entirely fortuitous and random, without any philosophical value. But there is no need even to make such metaphysical claims. It is enough to recognize that being *fated* to die is as if there were a dramatic author bestowing self-realization on his creatures. There is no knowledge claim here, simply an appeal to an image that makes the existential truth of our being fated comprehensible. We are not first believers and then, because of our beliefs, made meaningful; we are first meaningful and then, because our meaning is dependent on the worth of truth, we consider what existential presuppositions account for the thinkability of what this means. The story of our culture is not arbitrary; there are reasons why we think the way we do. Because truth matters, we are led to consider all critical possibilities that are consistent with our fate. To deny our fate would be a form of self-deception and therefore would be inconsistent with our concern for truth.

Accordingly, being mortal is, in itself, insufficient for our philosophical natures. We must realize we are *fated* to be mortal. But if this reasoning is correct, then fate is no longer mere appendage to our philosophical interests; it is fundamental. The contemporary neglect of the question of fate by our leading thinkers is a sad commentary on their distraction by the more abstract and hence more flattering issues. We are fated to die, and, although Epicurus's paradox may keep us from confronting death, we can reflect on the meaning of our finite existence. As fated beings, the meaning of fate is available to us. Similarly, as fated and finite, we can discover in the analysis of who we are what it means for truth to matter. The question "why me?" has finally led us, then, to the lodestone of all philosophical inquiry: the nature of truth.

12
■ ■ ■

TRUTH

Truth matters.

These two simple words, when conjoined to make this fundamental sentence, provide what may be the most critical presupposition of all thought. Certainly without this simple sentence the entire philosophical enterprise would be without warrant. Reflection on what this primordial sentence means may well be the most important of all philosophical tasks; for unless we understand *why* truth matters, we shall never be able to understand ourselves. Of all the various descriptions and definitions of our species, none equals the penetrative power suggested by this innocent claim: we are, in essence, beings for whom truth matters. The claim is not about knowledge, however. Aristotle's first sentence of the *Metaphysics* states, "All men by nature desire to know." But with all due respect to the great peripatetic, knowledge and truth are quite distinct in their meanings; to understand who we are as knowers is less fundamental, and hence misleading, than that we are, by our nature, those for whom and to whom truth matters.

Yet is the claim itself true? As a factual assertion it may be false. A paraphrase of Rousseau's opening sentence of *The Social Contract* is tempting: "Men are born truth-seekers, but everywhere they are beguiled by distraction." Perhaps the majority simply do not care about the truth. Indeed, observing their behavior, the persuasion is irresistible that few, if any, consider truth to matter at all. But such facts do not falsify the opening sentence of this chapter. Truth does matter, and it is only in appreciating the truth and meaning of this sentence that we can ever grasp what it means to be fated. It is our fate that truth matters. And only because truth matters can we be fated.

Even so, the claim that truth matters profoundly reveals something about the *meaning* of truth. If the opening sentence of this chapter is true, then we must understand truth itself as being able to matter. And this is sorely lacking in most traditional accounts of truth. For there is nothing in our understanding of, let us say, correspondence that would make it matter. There are times when knowledge of the correspondence might matter, but not correspondence by itself. How then, are we to understand truth as something that matters fundamentally? What is truth?

"What time is it?" someone asks, and a trustworthy companion responds, "A few minutes before three." The answer terminates the interrogative ignorance of the questioner. The truth of the answer satisfies why the question is asked. This is so obvious as to seem banal, but it is a point almost always overlooked and that when pressed reveals the original meaning of truth. Truth arrests. It halts. It is where the weary questioner can rest; it is, in other words, that which terminates and justifies asking. In the above example, if the response is from a trustworthy source we cannot possibly imagine the questioner asking again for the time, at least not right away.

But not all questions are resolved so completely. The true answer, "a few minutes before three," may indeed bring to a halt the interrogation about the time of day; but great questions cannot be so simply resolved. "What is gratitude?" simply does not permit of a response that terminates the question. Yet the truth of gratitude nevertheless provides a terminus, in the sense of an enclosure in which the continuing inquiry into its meaning can occur. In *Truth and Existence* I therefore suggest the distinction between the *true* and the *truth,* in which the former terminates by the providing of knowledge and the latter provides a terminus in which the meaning is enclosed, and by this enclosure the meaning unfolds or reveals. But in either case, the true or the truth terminates or encloses the questioning. Truth is that which, in confronting it, permits of no further advance. Thus truth entices, thereby provoking the questioning; but it also provides an arrest, thereby resolving, or at least enlightening, the questioning. In this way, truth not only matters; it is the ultimate presupposition that allows for any mattering whatsoever.

To say that truth matters is not to add on something new, as if the idea of truth could possibly not matter; the claim asserts no synthetic predication. The very understanding of what truth is must already contain the notion that it matters. (For if mattering were not an essential quality to truth, to assert that truth matters would be both contingent and relative, and the addendum "to whom?" would have to be inserted.) To realize that truth is the terminus to all thought incorporates 'mattering' into the very essence of truth.

But what do we *do* with truth? The search is for the proper verb or verbs. Do we *know* the truth? *Search* for it? *Worship* it? If truth really is the terminus of thought, perhaps we *confront* it. This confrontation can be concretized in four ways: I affirm, accept, acknowledge, and submit to truth. That is, to *affirm* truth is to say "yes" to it; it is to rejoice or to take pleasure in finally ending the quest. To *accept* truth is to yield to its power regardless of its impact, as when one accepts an argument superior to the one believed before or when the weight of evidence compels us to yield to the truth supported by these reasons. To *acknowledge* truth is to assimilate it as one's own, to embrace it as part of oneself, as in the acknowledgment of guilt. And, finally, to *submit* to truth is to surrender to its allure, as one enthralled by beauty cannot resist the seduction of its promise. In these four ways truth becomes pleasure, fate, guilt, and beauty. In confronting truth in these four ways, one affirms, accepts, acknowledges, and submits to truth. Truth, therefore, fundamentally matters; indeed truth is that which makes 'mattering' possible at all.

This four-fold account of truth as confrontation is more fully developed in my book *Truth and Existence,* and hence there is no need to defend this account in the present discussion. Attention is drawn, however, to the second of these four confrontations in which fate is revealed as a face of truth. If truth *arrests* in the sense of providing a terminus for the questioner, it can easily be seen why the response to our title question "why me?" must be given terminally (truthfully) "because it is my fate." By this we mean that there is no justification, no appeal beyond this tribunal, no metaphysical account, whether it be nature, purpose, or God's goodness. To ask "why me?" deserves an answer in truth: "because of who I am." The truth and the fate simply arrest, as a policeman stops the fugitive criminal on the warrant of reason. You can go no further. This arrest ends the flight from the law. The shackles are placed on our ankles, impeding us from escape. We are enclosed in a punitive cell.

The enclosure in the cell, however, gives us a place, a home, an arena in which our fugitive natures continue to pace and to explore the very walls and bars of enclosure, being denied the open fields. This incarceration encloses in on ourselves, focusing our probing lamps on our own reality. We continue to inquire, for truth is not like knowledge; it does not terminate the search but simply puts limiting walls around it, turning it on itself but not placating its hunger.

It is precisely because "why me?" has no *justificatory* answer that it brings the question to a halt. Why me? *I do not know*. Yet because the question is legitimate, the halting does not terminate my wonder, and so, denied justification, I seek illumination. The walls of enclosure that isolate me from the realm of satisfying answers in knowledge give a local habitation to my fugitive inquiry, providing a home in which illumination replaces justification. The acceptance, albeit enforced, of this is the fated confrontation of truth and the imprisoned realization that truth itself is fateful.

Fate is therefore a face of truth just because in halting the inquiry it permits of no further inquisition beyond itself but demands acceptance. Yet truth itself is fateful because it unfolds our reality as who we are, in narrative inevitability. But to recognize this in no way justifies unearned suffering or undeserved favor. In no way does it solve practical problems or inform us of metaphysical entities. It does not tell us how we should live our lives or even how we should adopt attitudes for achieving the proper psychological outlook for success in dealing with the vagaries of fortune. Rather these realizations guide only our thinking, and thereby our nearness to truth. As thinkers, and not as mere calculators, truth matters. Truth does not matter because of its use, or power, or even because it promises theological salvation. Truth matters absolutely; that is, it needs no justification whatsoever. To seek to justify truth is necessarily to misunderstand it.

We are fated to revere truth, that is, the unfolding of our story. But since it is *our* story, in spite of its uselessness it is of supreme preciousness. Truth is precious because it is ours. Simultaneously, we are who we are because of truth. Thus, it is the *thinkability* of who we are that makes our fated truth and our true fate worthy of our effort. Were truth not the final, ultimate cessation of our questioning, not in the sense of stopping our thinking but in making it worthwhile by enclosing it, we would be entirely unanchored, a floating, meaningless, and indifferent capacity for infinite possibility. Fated, we are rendered finite, and only as finite can we think. Only

as finite are we ourselves. But finitude, by its very defini-
tional essence, cannot be entirely self-justified. There must
be an unknowable bestowal that, ever beyond the powers of
our reason to justify, can nevertheless be affirmed, accepted,
acknowledged, and submitted to. Since it is beyond our capacity to *know*, but not beyond our capacity to think about, it
is our fate.

God, if there be one, in knowing all, has no fate; and as
such, neither does He confront truth. There is no truth for
the divine, for as all-powerful nothing stops Him, nothing encloses Him. Fate and truth are reserved for thinkers; truth
and fate are meaningful only for the finite. Bestowed, fated,
and abandoned, we are unfolded in the truth of our told stories whose beginning and end enclose our meaning. We learn
much in the reflection of this unfolding drama that is ourselves. We can affirm it, accept it, acknowledge it, and submit
to its allure and its inevitability. And the reason is radiant: we
matter because truth matters.

www.ingramcontent.com/pod-product-compliance
Ingram Content Group UK Ltd.
Pitfield, Milton Keynes, MK11 3LW, UK
UKHW030942090325
455861UK00003B/11